Is

zy!

Hell

Jessica

Adams Media

Avon, Massachusetts

Published by
Adams Media, an F+W Publications Company
57 Littlefield Street, Avon, MA 02322. U.S.A.
www.adamsmedia.com

ISBN: 1-59337-269-8

Printed in Canada.
J I H G F E D C B A

Library of Congress Cataloging-in-Publication Data
Fee, Susan.
My roommate is driving me crazy! / Susan Fee.
p.   cm.
ISBN 1-59337-269-8
1. Roommates. I. Title.
HQ975.F44 2005
646.7′0088′378198—dc22
2005007442

This publication is designed to provide accurate and authoritative information
with regard to the subject matter covered. It is sold with the understanding that
the publisher is not engaged in rendering legal, accounting, or other professional
advice. If legal advice or other expert assistance is required, the services of a
competent professional person should be sought.
    —From a *Declaration of Principles* jointly adopted by a Committee of the
American Bar Association and a Committee of Publishers and Associations

Many of the designations used by manufacturers and sellers to distinguish
their products are claimed as trademarks. Where those designations appear in
this book and Adams Media was aware of a trademark claim, the designations
have been printed with initial capital letters.

Illustration by Dave Winter.

This book is available at quantity discounts for bulk purchases.
For information, call 1-800-872-5627.

Dedication

This book is dedicated to my husband, Allan. Thank you for being the kindest, most loving, and most supportive roommate I'll ever have! And to my daughter Gabrielle, may you never need this book! But, if you do, know that your mom and dad love and support you 100 percent.

Acknowledgments

This book would never have happened if it were not for the coolest boss in the world: Dr. Jim Nolan. You gave me a chance, listened to my ideas, and encouraged me in a way that every person in the world should be blessed enough to experience.

My deepest gratitude also goes to the entire staff of the Baldwin-Wallace Health and Counseling Center in Berea, Ohio. I've never attended a better potluck! In particular I must thank Luis Rosa, Dr. Victoria Kress, Theresa Novak, and Dr. Stephanie Ford, whose insight and feedback were invaluable. To the students and clients who trusted me with your stories and who agreed to read my rough drafts, I am indebted. Rachael Mattis, I asked you to give me honest feedback, and you did. It may have been brutal at times, but it was right on the money. You are a goddess!

To the Residence Life Directors and staff from across the country who answered my interview questions, provided examples, and offered feedback—I hope this book saves you some future headaches! Thanks to Sarah Scott Hall, Cara Brumby, Derek Steele, Julia Andrews, Corey King, Linda Short, and Brandie Plasket.

Every writer needs friends she can call in the eleventh hour of desperation. For me those people are Dr. Amanda Costin, Dr. Rose Quinones-DelValle, Andrea Peck, and Anna Sarrocco, all wise, wonderful women.

Finally, to my agent, Catherine Fowler, who signed me based on an idea and a colleague's good word, thanks for your leap of faith. Kristin Nelson, thanks for putting in that good word!

Contents

Introduction

There's nothing like waking up in the middle of the night to the sounds of your college roommate having sex in the bunk above you. What about the roommate who secretly borrows your things? Then there's the neat freak who alphabetizes canned goods and the person who won't talk, but sends you instant messages from his computer four feet away. These can be the roommates from hell!

When you filled out your roommate questionnaire, you probably didn't bargain for this. Maybe you played it safe and roomed with your best friend. Now the two of you barely speak. What happens when your quad mates turn on you? What do you say when your roommate tells you she is gay? How do you handle gossip? Stealing?

As a college counselor and adjunct professor, I've heard every one of these stories and more. Conflicts usually heat up mid-semester when room transfers are hard to get. Trying to find a place off campus in a hurry can be costly and stressful. Most students have to bite the bullet and deal, which, quite frankly, is what your college or university expects of you. But, if you don't know how, life can seem unbearable. When you're experiencing a living hell, it can affect your emotional well-being, mental concentration, academic performance, and relationships. I wrote this book to save you some of that pain and to show you that you're not alone. All of the stories and examples in this book are from real students who were willing to share their horror stories with me. Some names have been changed to protect students' privacy, and some stories are a compilation of several situations. You may recognize your own story within these pages.

After talking to and counseling a countless number of students, I discovered that most of their roommate situations could be improved at least a little, if not a lot, with the kind of guidance offered in this book. You can't change or control other people. If you're living with a jerk, there's no guarantee he will suddenly transform. But you can influence your situation by how you respond. If nothing else, you'll find enough ideas in this book to get you through the semester until you can make other housing arrangements.

Another thing I've learned from helping students is that most of them *hate* conflict and confrontation. They'll do anything to avoid it. Unfortunately that only makes the problem worse. If confrontation leaves you tongue-tied, don't worry because I did the prep work for you. I've included specific examples of exactly what to say in the toughest situations, like how to tell your roommate his B.O. is making you gag! You'll find several conversation starters for every conflict situation and a few more you can use if your first efforts need some backup. So if your roommate didn't get the hint about cleaning up dirty dishes, you'll have plenty of ideas on how to bring it up again.

One area that tends to get overlooked is mental health. What do you do if your roommate threatens suicide? Are you aware of the signs of depression? Eating disorders are prevalent in college-age students too, and drug and alcohol use can reach scary levels. It can be incredibly stressful living with someone who is unable to make reasonable decisions and who needs professional help. That's why most campuses have counseling centers that offer services for free or a nominal charge. These are serious issues. I've given you guidelines on what you can do if you think your roommate is in trouble.

So whether your problem is that you're living with your total opposite, never getting your phone messages, or are always hungry because someone is eating your food, you'll find solutions in this book. If things still don't improve after trying everything within these pages, you will even find tips here on how and when to break things off without making the situation worse. Don't let the roommate from hell ruin your life one more day!

I'd love to hear how your story turns out. Please visit my Web site at *www.susanfee.com*, and let me know.

1

What Did You Expect?

Quick Quiz: True or False

My living situation is nothing like I expected.　　　　T/F

I assumed my roommate would at least be reasonable.　T/F

If I had known it would turn out like this, I would

have chosen a different roommate.　　　　　　　　　T/F

Score:

1 T: The closest thing you have to *Friends* is watching it in syndication.

2 Ts: The couch in the lounge is sounding pretty good right now.

3 Ts: You asked the Army recruiter how soon you could enter boot camp.

Toto, We're Not in Kansas Anymore

"I knew my roommate before we lived together. She seemed really nice, so I assumed we'd hang out together or talk. But it's nothing like that. She's a lot different than I thought she'd be. Now, we can barely stand to look at one another."

—JAMIE, AGE 18

Do you ever look at your roommate and wonder, "Who is this person?" "What am I doing here?" "How can I get out of this mess?" Whatever your situation, it's probably not what you expected, especially if you've always had your own room and private bath and have never lived in such close quarters with anybody. It might have sounded cool to room with a foreign exchange student at first, until you realized you had nothing in common. Or maybe you played it safe and roomed with your best friend, but now you're living with tape down the middle of the room. Maybe you agreed to share food only to find out your roomie never buys any! When you expect one thing and get another, it can be a shock. It can also be disappointing because you were prepared mentally and emotionally for something else. Even the greatest of relationships have conflict. *Expecting* to have disagreements is a lot different than assuming you'll never have a fight. The bigger the gap is between what you expected and the unpleasant reality of the situation, the higher your stress level. You can bridge that gap by learning to adapt your expectations. That doesn't mean you have to lower all of your standards, but you may have to adjust a few.

I Wasn't Expecting You

So what are reasonable roommate expectations, and what do you need to let go of? Check yourself against these lists to see where you may have to make some adjustments.

It's OK to Expect . . .

Personal safety. You have the right to feel safe in your living space at all times.

Respectful communication. No shouting, name calling, or vicious e-mails.

Respect for your personal property. No using your things without your permission.

Rules that are made together. One person doesn't get to decide all of them.

Conflict. Yes, *expect* it because it's normal to have differences.

Compromise. Both of you will have to give up something at some point.

You Shouldn't Expect That . . .

Your roommate will be your best friend. Some people end up being friends, but most just share a space, and that's it.

Your roommate will keep you company. It's easy to use a roommate as a social crutch when you're lonely or bored. However, it's not your roommate's job to entertain or hang out with you.

You'll have something in common with your roommate. You may be going to the same school, but everyone's different.

Your roommate will listen to you and do what you want. We have no control over other people and their behavior.

You'll always get along with your roommate. It's impossible to agree with someone 100 percent of the time.

Your roommate must make all the changes because you're "right." Compromise means that both of you will need to adapt.

Reality Check

"My roommate and I used to do everything together. Then he got a girl-friend who's really controlling. He's not allowed to spend any time with his guy friends anymore, or he gets in trouble. Now I don't have anyone to hang out with."

—JOSH, AGE 18

If you're hanging onto the dream of what you thought would happen (and it's clearly not happening) here's a reality check. Nothing can change until you accept what *is*, instead of what *was supposed to be*. Your roommate is probably going through the same thing. This can make the tension in the room build to the point where it feels like you can't even breathe. The situation can improve by being honest with yourself and your roommate about what you expected and what you didn't.

One of the first things you must accept is that you can't control other people. As much as you may want to fix your roommate or force her to change, it's not your responsibility. Conversely, it's not okay for anyone else to try to control you. When one person tries to decide what's right and wrong or good and bad for somebody else, the conflict turns from bad to worse.

How to Break the Ice

Just because you can't control your roommate doesn't mean your situation is hopeless and nothing can change! A lot can change depending on the way you respond, the conversations you have, and the limits you set. If your reality is nothing like what you expected, here are some examples of how you can start a conversation with your roommate to ease the tension:

1. "I thought things were going to be different. It would mean a lot to me if we could talk about how things can improve."
2. "This is totally different than I expected. How did you picture it?"
3. "Honestly, living with someone else is a lot harder than I thought it would be. Is this what you expected?"

4. "Being away at school is hard! It's a lot different than I imagined. I think I need some time to adjust."

5. "I can see now that I assumed some things that I shouldn't have. What about you?"

6. "I don't know about you, but this feels really uncomfortable. It's not what I thought it would be."

The first thing to do in any type of conflict with your roommate is to acknowledge it exists. Sometimes that, in and of itself, is enough to open up communication and improve the situation.

My Roommate Has Totally Different Expectations

If you're not getting along with your roommate, it's likely that both of you had different ideas of what it would be like to live together. Conflicts begin when you operate on assumptions that don't exist for the other person. The good news is that by discovering your differences, you can begin to address problems. Talking about them can clear the air, even if nothing changes. Sometimes, just acknowledging out loud what's going on is a relief.

Now I Get It!

Avoid labeling your roommate's expectations as wrong or stupid by saying something like, "How the heck did you ever get that idea?" You don't have to agree with the other person—you just have to hear him out. If you find out you are coming from a completely different place than your roommate, here's how you can respond:

1. "Now it makes sense that we've been arguing. I had no idea you saw it that way."
2. "I'm surprised to hear how differently we think about this."
3. "I had no idea you expected things to be so different."
4. "Wow, I can see why we're not getting along. We were thinking totally opposite things."
5. "No wonder we disagree. Now I hear where you're coming from."
6. "I think I understand why we've been getting on each other's nerves. We had different expectations."

Remember, we tend to create assumptions or expectations of people based on our needs, not those of the other person. Maybe you expected your roommate to eat dinner with you every night because you're homesick or lonely. That's a lot of pressure to put on one person! Look at where you may have taken things for granted because you wanted or needed her to be a certain way.

Best Friends, Worst Enemies

"My best friend and I decided to live together. What a mistake! I never realized how hard it would be to be around her all the time. We fight so much that I'm afraid we won't be friends after this."

—DANA, AGE 19

There's close, and then there's *too* close. It's amazing how quickly the quirky things you used to like about your best friend begin to drive you crazy. It makes sense to expect that rooming with a person whom you know so well would be a good thing. But knowing too much about your roommate can also have its drawbacks. College is about growing and making new friends. Only hanging out with your best friend can hold both of you back. All it takes is one, "You didn't used to be that way," to feel trapped. There are only so many times you can re-tell old high school stories!

Another mistake made by best friends is assuming they don't have to set any ground rules. A roommate relationship takes friendship to a whole other level because now it involves sharing space, time, and decision-making. If you don't establish boundaries with your friend like you would with someone you don't know as well, it's too easy to cross the line. You can end up feeling taken advantage of because you assumed your friend would make the same decisions as you, even though it was never discussed.

How to Break the Ice

Even though you and your friend have a history together, you still need to talk about how you envision your living situation, or else someone's feelings may get hurt. Here is what you can say if rooming with your best friend is driving you apart instead of bringing you closer together:

1. "Our friendship means a lot to me, and I feel like living together is putting a strain on it. How about we do some more things with other friends so we can give each other a break?"

2. "You're one of my best friends, but I feel like we're holding each other back. Why don't we try hanging out with other people for awhile?"

3. "High school was fun, but I want to experience college now. I feel like we keep bringing up the past instead of moving forward."

4. "I still want to be friends, but I think it would be healthy for me to have some space right now."

5. "I don't want to ruin our friendship by wearing it out. What if we try to meet some new people?"

Be gentle when asking for some space. Your friend may be hurt initially—especially if he doesn't see the constant closeness as a problem. Re-emphasize how much the friendship means to you, and give your friend patience and understanding if he needs to work through any hurt feelings.

Our Friendship Is Already in the Dumps

It's hard to believe that living together can ruin a friendship, but it can happen. A few choice words and unfortunate conversations can put your friendship to the test. It's also possible to outgrow a friendship because you're both going in different directions, even though you thought you were so alike. It's hard to predict everything you're going to experience in college and how you'll react. Some people end up drifting apart.

Future Friends . . . Maybe?

Your friendship being on the rocks now doesn't cancel out the good times you had before. And it doesn't necessarily mean that the two of you won't be on the same path again in time. If there are hurt feelings, it's important to clear the air. Then shift your expectations. Make it your goal to be compatible roommates instead of being best friends. If you need help making the transition, here's what you can say:

1. "It feels weird that we were so close, and now we can't even talk without arguing. But I still think we can live together if we lighten up a little."

2. "You've been a good friend, and even though we're fighting right now, I still appreciate that."

3. "It's cool that we're finding out we're into different things. College is the time when we're supposed to figure out who we are."

4. "Our friendship is strained because we're going in different directions. That doesn't mean we can't live together—just not with the same expectations as before."

Long-term relationships go through many adjustments. If you and your friend have never had to confront any issues, then dealing with your problems as roommates can be rough. If you can work through them, you may find that it makes your friendship stronger than ever. If not, then you may need to let go of a friendship that no longer serves who you are now.

Detour Ahead

Okay, so things aren't going exactly as you planned. This is a real test of your patience and flexibility (or lack thereof). If you find yourself repeating, "I can't believe this is happening," or, "This isn't how it was supposed to be," you're in denial. It is happening. Let go of Plan A, and move on to Plan B. Don't have a Plan B? Now is the time to get one!

Adjusting Your Game Plan

So you don't have the perfect roommate relationship. That doesn't have to make you miserable. The more you can learn to ride the waves, the easier you'll make it on yourself. If you're not comfortable with change or have trouble being flexible, here are some tips:

Think big picture. This is not a permanent situation. You're not stuck with your roommate for the rest of your life. In semester terms, it's a matter of weeks.

Shift your focus. If you concentrate on everything your roommate does that irritates you, it'll just get worse. Focus on the not-so-bad or neutral times.

Step off the "perfect" pedestal. Human beings are flawed, we have differences, and because of that, we argue. Expecting a perfect relationship with your roommate (or anyone else) is way too much pressure, not to mention impossible.

Build new skills. This book is filled with ideas on how to improve your situation. Adjusting your expectations is just the first step. Don't stop until you've tried them all.

Have a back-up plan. Know ahead of time what you'll do when your roommate is driving you nuts. Of course you don't want to reinforce negative behaviors by leaving every time your roommate is inconsiderate, but it's helpful to know you have a place to go if you need it. If your roommate makes studying in the room impossible, come up with other locations. If your roommate occasionally invites tons of people over when you want to sleep, have another place you can go. Of course it's not ideal, but knowing you have an escape route will keep you in control.

Tips to Remember

- The bigger the gap is between your expectations and reality, the higher your stress level.
- Reasonable roommate expectations include personal safety, respectful communication, respect for your property, and willingness to compromise. It's *not* reasonable to expect your roommate to be your best friend or hang out with you.
- You can't control other people. Expecting others to change for you leads to disappointment.
- Best friends don't always make the best roommates. College is a time to grow and develop new friendships.
- If your situation is nothing like you expected, move to Plan B. Keeping the big picture in mind will make it easier. Remember that your roommate situation is not permanent.

You can also learn more about roommate relationships by visiting your campus counseling center or by checking out *www.campusblues.com*. If you think things couldn't be any worse, prepare yourself with tips from *Worst-Case Scenario Survival Handbook: College* (Chronicle Books, 2004).

2

Houston, We Have a Problem

Pick Your Battles

*"My roommate and I fight about everything, but the main thing that bugs
me is when she eats my food and then lies about it. Sometimes I even
wonder if it's worth bringing up since it doesn't seem to make a difference
anyway."*

—ALISON, AGE 22

It's no fun being in a constant battle with your roommate. After awhile
you might wonder, is this worth it? Good question. Some battles are
definitely *not* worth it. Everyone's allowed to make mistakes or to be in
a bad mood once in awhile. If you're fighting over differences of opin-

ion when the outcome really doesn't impact your life one way or the other, you don't need to start dumping your roommate's clothes out the window. Let it go! You can't control other people's opinions anyway, so don't waste your time and energy. You and your roommate don't have to agree on every point to get along.

Think about your other living options. Knowing that you're stuck with your roommate for the rest of the semester or longer will help you to decide what you can and can't tolerate. An issue that initially seems worth fighting for may not be that big a deal if you have nowhere else to go.

Don't Sit This One Out

Issues become a big deal when they cross into personal territory. For instance, your roommate borrowing your stuff without asking, using substances in the room that could get you kicked out, or not paying the phone bill on time are all issues that affect you negatively and should be addressed. If your roommate has done any of the following, consider it a red flag:

- Threatening physical harm
- Assaulting you verbally (yelling, screaming, swearing)
- Stealing from you
- Damaging your personal property
- Breaking living or lease agreements in a way that could get you kicked out or that jeopardizes your credit or deposit
- Not paying bills or rent on time
- Ignoring your personal space
- Invading your privacy

If your roommate is acting in a way that violates your safety, property, personal rights, or living agreement (see Chapter 6), then it's time to stand up for yourself.

I Win, You Lose

"My roommate has such a big ego that he has to be right about every-thing. He won't compromise or change his mind because he never thinks he's wrong. Any disagreement we have is a fight to the bitter end."

—RON, AGE 21

Some people just don't know how to fight fairly! Their idea of having a "discussion," is telling you all about how they're right and you're wrong. Bet you didn't think that in addition to lectures from parents and professors, you'd have to hear 'em from your roommate, too! If you're dealing with an attitude of my-way-or-the-highway, you're dealing with unreasonable expectations. The only way for things to work out is to accept that neither one of you gets to be right 100 percent of the time.

Someone who is trying to win every argument is not trying to compromise. Makes sense, right? Here's the tricky part: it sounds good to say you're going to approach your problem with a "win-win" attitude, where both of you get something out of the deal. But, the reality is that in order for your roommate to win, you have to lose! No ties, only winner takes all. It's like trying to play three sets of tennis with a win-win approach; someone is going to end up with more points. So, what do you do? When you're dealing with someone whose competitive nature compels him to win all the time, change the game. Give up on winning and go for what's *fair*.

Being fair means negotiating tradeoffs. For example, if your roommate hogs the couch and TV, but you don't care about TV anyway, then it's not really fair to split viewing rights 50-50. Instead, let your roommate have permanent TV rights for something you really want—like more closet space.

Give up trying to make everybody happy, because to do that, both of you would have things totally your way—not happening! If you consider uttering the words, "Are you happy now?" slap yourself silly! Fair does not always equal happy, and it's not your place to have to make other people happy.

How to Break the Ice

There's a good chance your roommate will never be fully satisfied, so don't even try. However, there are some tactics you can use. Here's how to approach your roommate with a fair-fair mindset:

1. "I think we both agree that this is not our ideal situation, so let's figure out what's fair."
2. "We both want to be right, but that's not getting us anywhere. What do you think is fair?"
3. "Deciding what's fair doesn't mean it will be perfect for either of us, but at least we can move on."
4. "Instead of arguing about who is right, let's talk about what's fair."
5. "Since we both can't have everything we want, let's just focus on what's fair."

Trying to work things out with a goal of being fair to both sides takes the pressure off having to come up with a solution where both of you get everything you want. (Hey, if you could do that, you wouldn't be fighting!)

My Roommate Won't Budge

Dealing with someone who won't compromise can be incredibly frustrating. But it's important to stay cool because getting too emotional will put you on the losing end for sure. The more frustrated you appear, the more you'll fuel the fire.

There are two reasons your roommate could be stalling. First, he is still stuck on being right. So let your roommate score a win. Pick something minor that really doesn't matter to you (but of course don't tell that to your roomie!). You don't have to say he is right on everything, and be sure it's not a pivotal issue. Second, he isn't really suffering compared to you. If your roommate is experiencing only minimal inconveniences or consequences, there's no need to change. That puts you in a more desperate position. Be careful that you're not so accommodating that you're making it easy for the other person to have it all.

You're Right!

Here are some suggestions for getting a stubborn person to compromise without sounding like you're kissing butt:

1. "I agree with you on your first point, and I especially don't want to argue anymore. How do you want to figure this out so it's fair?"

2. "You're so right that this needs to change. How about we

come up with a plan that'll work for both of us?"

3. "I agree with you, and I'm tired of fighting too. Now all we have to figure out is what's fair."

4. "I think you're right about this, so we don't need to keep fighting about it. Let's focus on coming up with a fair plan."

5. "Yes, you're right on this one. How about we move on to solving the rest of our problems?"

Sometimes the person just needs to hear the words, "You're right," before agreeing to anything else! If you look at it as helping you get what you want in the end, then a little strategic ego massaging isn't such a bad thing.

What's Your Problem?

"Sometimes my roommate and I get into it, and after awhile, I don't even know what we're fighting about. We say mean things and talk in circles. Then one of us storms out yelling 'Fine!' and slams the door behind us."

—LIZ, AGE 19

The first step in solving any disagreement is to define the problem. As obvious as it sounds, you'll be surprised to learn that your roommate has a different perspective than you about the situation. It's really hard to solve a problem if you can't even agree on what it is! The main reason misunderstandings occur is that each of us bases reality on our own perceptions, which is our personal, unique filtering system. Even though it may seem like you and your roommate are fighting about the same thing, you're actually viewing it through separate lenses that distort the information. Our perception supports what we believe to be true and minimizes everything else.

How to Break the Ice

In order to problem solve, both sides need to understand the other's perception of what's going on. Hear the other person out completely without argument (that includes no eye-rolling or heavy sighs), and then tell your side of the story. Here are some ways you can begin to understand where your roommate is coming from:

1. "I know what I think is going on, but I want to understand it from your perspective. What do you think is the problem?"
2. "Obviously we don't agree, but I'm not sure we fully understand one another's reasons. Will you tell me your side?"
3. "We each have our own version of the problem, and I want to understand where you're coming from. Will you tell me?"
4. "I want to get a handle on the real problem. I promise to listen to you without interrupting if you'll listen to me."
5. "Let's take it from the top. Tell me why you're upset."

The only way to get the other person's point of view is to ask! Don't worry about solving anything at this point; just get both sides of the story.

We Have Two Different Problems

If your roommate's description of the problem is totally different from yours, then agree to work on both. Avoid putting down his version by saying, "That's not the issue" or "That's not even a big deal," because then you will have started a totally new argument. Start by solving the easiest issue first. At least then you know that you both can agree on *something* before tackling the tougher stuff.

See Eye to Eye

Here's how you can respond if your roommate's perception of the problem is different than your own:

1. "No wonder we've been fighting so much, we're arguing about two different things. Now that we each know what the other is thinking, which problem do you want to work on first?"

2. "I had no idea you thought that was the problem. I think we both have a point, but let's deal with the easiest problem first."

3. "Both of us need an answer to what we think is the problem. It sounds like yours is easier to deal with, so let's solve that one first. Then we can talk about mine."

4. "I get where you're coming from now. Which problem should we work on first?"

5. "I guess we have two issues to deal with, but I think one of them sounds pretty easy to take care of right now."

6. "Let's work on both problems. How about we get the easy one out of the way?"

Don't worry about whose problem is justified or more important. Everybody has the right to her own perceptions, so give attention to both sides of the argument.

It Takes Two to Tango

"I come up with all sorts of ideas on how my roommate and I can solve our problems, but no matter what I say, she puts them down. I'm tired of trying so hard to work it out, when she doesn't put forth any effort."

—LINDSEY, AGE 18

It takes at least two people to create a disagreement and at least two people to solve it. But sometimes, one person becomes super-motivated to fix it and ends up taking over. If you're the type of person who likes to generate ideas on how your roommate issue can be solved, you may be frustrated when your ideas are rejected or, at the very least, not met with enthusiasm. No matter how good your ideas are, you may be set up to fail because people don't like to be told what to do. You want to come across as helpful, but your roommate feels like you're acting like a parent trying to boss around a child.

People tend to dismiss solutions that they've had no say in creating. Even if your roommate agrees to one of your ideas for awhile, it may not stick. Sometimes it's easier to agree to something in the moment just to get the other person to be quiet. If you really want a compromise that both of you will commit to, then both of you need to be involved in brainstorming the solution. That means your ultimate solution could be a plan neither one of you would have suggested on your own, but is something new created together.

How to Break the Ice

On the surface, it sounds like a great idea to approach your roommate with a bunch of ideas. But it may seem to him that you've already figured out the "right" way to handle things, so why bother taking part? Here's what you can say to encourage him to work with you on finding the best solution for both of you:

1. "Now that we both understand what we want, what are your ideas on how we can compromise?"
2. "What if we both agree to one thing we'd be willing to compromise on, and then see if that helps us think of a plan?"
3. "It's important we come up with a solution we can both live with, so what if we each make one suggestion at a time and see where that gets us?"
4. "What if I tell you one thing I'm willing to give on, then you tell me one thing you're willing to give on?"
5. "I have an idea for how we might solve this, but I'd like to hear what you think first."
6. "What do you feel is the most important thing that needs to be addressed?"

She'll tune you out if you say, "I know exactly what we should do!" or "I've come up with a plan." Ask your roommate for her ideas first, or suggest that both of you come up with the same number of possible solutions to discuss.

My Roommate Is Two-Faced

You may think you've worked things out, but then your roommate doesn't keep up his side of the bargain. A couple of things could be going on. First, make sure your roommate feels the solution is truly mutual and not something you dictated. Remember, if both of you don't create it together, then the other person has nothing invested in its outcome. Second, your roommate may not have been honest from the start about what he thinks is the real problem. People who are uncomfortable with conflict sometimes bluff their way through discussions because it feels too uncomfortable to face the real issue.

Call Her Out on It

The more both of you have at stake, the more you'll be motivated to follow through. If your roommate is saying one thing and doing another, call her on it right away. Here is how you can approach the topic again:

1. "I thought we had an agreement, but it won't work if each of us doesn't hold up her end of the bargain. Have you changed your mind about something?"

2. "Is there something we agreed to that's not working for you now? I think it's only fair that we either follow through or change it."

3. "I get the feeling that you agreed to something in the moment, but that's not how you really feel. Is there something else bugging you?"

4. "This is feeling one-sided. When I agreed to this, I assumed you'd follow through too."

5. "I think we need to start over again and decide what's fair and what's not. We also need to figure out what we think should happen if one of us backs out."

Finally, the solution the two of you create needs to have built-in consequences for not following through. If your roommate goes back on her word and suffers nothing as a result, why change? Decide from the start what the consequences will be if either side drops the ball. For example, maybe someone has to give up her TV rights, or allow the other to have the room to herself on a certain night. Or, you could donate equal amounts to a cash pot, and whoever breaks the agreement forfeits the money.

Tips to Remember

- Pick and choose your battles. Let minor differences of opinions go, but—again—never ignore violations of your safety, your privacy, your personal rights or space, or your lease/living agreement that may penalize you.
- Instead of fighting to win, settle on what's fair.
- If your roommate refuses to compromise, he may feel the need to be controlling. If your roommate insists on being "right," give up a win on a minor issue to get the ball rolling.
- Before you can solve the problem, you need to agree on what it is. Your roommate may have a completely different perception than you do, and the only way to find out is to ask.
- Collaborate on solutions. If one roommate comes up with all the ideas, the other person will resent it.

If you want to learn more about problem solving, visit your campus counseling center or check out the conflict resolution Web site created by the University of Wisconsin-Madison at *www.obrd.wisc.edu/onlinetraining/resolution*. If you have conflict all the time, read *Don't Sweat the Small Stuff and It's All Small Stuff: Simple Ways to Keep the Little Things from Taking Over Your Life* by Richard Carlson (Hyperion, 1997).

3

I'm Not Good at Confrontation

Quick Quiz: True or False

Just the thought of confronting your roommate gives
you sweaty palms and butterflies in your stomach.   T/F

You'd rather endure three hours of fingernails on a
blackboard than confront your roommate.   T/F

It's easier to give in than to argue for what you
really want.   T/F

Score:

1 T: You've purchased so many antacids you could be the
company spokesperson.

2 Ts: You've started wearing sunglasses to avoid eye contact
with your roommate.

3 Ts: The only communication you have with your roommate is when you read each other's blogs.

The Elephant in the Room

*"There isn't anything I hate more than fighting. I just want everyone to be
happy and work it out. It's easier to let my roommate have her way, even
if that means I don't ever get mine."*

—STEPHANIE, AGE 18

Most people avoid confrontation, not because of what happens, but
because of what they fear *might* happen. We imagine the worst-case
scenario, even if it has never actually occurred. If you've had a bad

experience in the past, you might assume the same thing will happen again next time. The anticipation alone can make you feel like hiding under the nearest rock. You can drive yourself crazy asking a lot of "what if" questions: What if my roommate freaks out on me? What if my roommate denies everything? The fear is not so much about what *we* might do, but rather how the other person might react.

Are You Avoiding Confrontation?

It's possible to have a lot more control over the situation than you may think just by adjusting your approach. The first step is confronting your own thoughts. Here are some common fears people have about confrontation; see if you can relate:

The other person will yell and scream at me.

I'll cry or get so emotional that I won't get my point across.

The other person will get physical and I may get hurt.

I'll be perceived as being too aggressive or not likeable.

I'll make the situation worse.

I can't say anything to change the situation anyway.

I'll forget what I want to say, or get tongue-tied.

I'll feel embarrassed.

I'll look like an idiot.

I'll be manipulated or proven wrong.

Think about the confrontations you've had in the past with parents, teachers, friends and/or boyfriends/girlfriends. What happened? How did you react or feel? Are those same feelings playing out now with your roommate?

Weighing the Pros and Cons

Do the fears just mentioned sound familiar? If you can identify with any or all of them, it's probably going to take some extra convincing to make you believe that confrontation can be a good thing! There are pros and cons to every situation. If your roommate is graduating next week, then it's probably not worth starting something. But, most likely your problem is not going to magically disappear any time soon. So, you have to consider the possible consequences of not dealing with the situation:

- Feeling stressed, angry, or resentful
- Getting sick frequently
- Feeling either overly tired or wired and anxious most of the time
- Having other relationships suffer
- Thinking about the situation constantly

It can be tough, but there are rewards for confronting an issue. There are no guarantees everything will work out since it takes your roommate's cooperation too, but you'll never know unless you try.

Confrontation Can Be Good!

Here are some positive benefits of facing the problem head-on:

- The problem gets solved
- You will feel a sense of relief
- Your pride and confidence will increase for taking the risk
- You will earn your roommate's respect

Confronting issues will make your relationship with your room-mate stronger, even if the two of you don't end up being friends. It will be easier to live with your roommate—and yourself.

Evening the Odds

"I've tried talking to my roommate a couple of times to work out our dif-ferences, but I never know what to expect. Sometimes he's cool and some-times he bites my head off. With him, I can't predict which way things are going to go."

—KUNAL, AGE 20

One of the scary things about bringing up a sensitive topic is that you're never quite sure how the other person will take it. If your room-mate goes off on you sometimes, but breaks down in tears or listens quietly during others, how do you know what's coming next? The roller coaster ride can be enough to keep you from wanting to say anything ever again. If every talk with your roommate feels like a gam-ble, then decide ahead of time how the game should be played.

Play Fair

Pick a time when things are calm and approach your roommate about setting up ground rules for how disagreements should be han-dled. If you can agree to these early on then you'll have something to fall back on if your roommate isn't fighting fair. For instance, if you both agree that neither of you will yell, you can refer back to the ear-lier agreement should your roommate start to get loud. Here are some suggestions for what it takes to have a fair discussion:

- Each person agrees that it's a good time to talk.
- No interrupting.
- Restate or paraphrase what the other person said to make sure you understand.
- Be accountable for opinions and feelings using "I" statements. (For example, "I really get angry when dirty dishes are left in the sink.")
- No attacking the other person with "you" statements. (For example, "You never clean up your dishes.")
- No yelling, screaming, swearing, or name-calling.
- No complaining without making at least one suggestion for how to do things differently.

Also, never walk out in the middle of a discussion; it is fair to call for a time out if things get too heated, as long as you agree to come back and finish the discussion later.

How to Break the Ice

Remember to bring up issues when things are calm rather than in the middle of an argument. Here's how you can start a conversation about how to fight fair:

1. "I'd like to agree up front on how we're going to work out any disagreements."
2. "Just in case something comes up between us, how do you think we should handle it?"
3. "I think it would be easier to agree now how we want to settle future problems instead of in the heat of the moment."

4. "How about we figure out now what we're going to do when we disagree."

The more you know what to expect, the easier it will be to talk to your roommate about a difficult situation. You might even want to write down what the two of you decide.

My Roommate Isn't Holding to His End of the Bargain

It's easy to say you'll be reasonable when you're calm, but it's much harder to actually do it when you're mad. If your roommate pulls a bait-and-switch by agreeing to fight fair, then breaks all the rules, stick to your original plan. No matter what happens, the fact is he already agreed with you about how to work out problems. If your roommate starts yelling or interrupting you, bring up your earlier agreement. If it continues, stop talking until he calms down.

Nip It in the Bud

Here's how you can respond if your roommate goes from agreeable to disagreeable:

1. "We already came up with a plan as to how we'd talk about this kind of stuff. Since we agreed, let's stick to it."
2. "We already covered this stuff when we agreed to fight fair. Let's not backtrack."
3. "This isn't how we said we were going to handle things during an argument."

4. "I thought we agreed to certain ground rules. Wouldn't it be easier to use them?"

It's very possible that your roommate could be testing your limits. If you allow the rules to be changed mid-argument, then your roommate will know that you can be easily persuaded. We teach people how to treat us. If your roommate knows he can walk over you once, chances are he will look for a second opportunity down the road.

Cut the Bull(y)

"I don't like confrontation because I don't want to come off as aggressive. I don't think acting like a bully is going to solve anything."
—MITCH, AGE 20

If your definition of confrontation includes being aggressive or bullying the other person, then put on the armor and get ready to fight! The only thing aggressive behavior does is trigger the other person's defenses to fight back. That doesn't really solve anything. Aggressive people know no boundaries; they stomp all over other people just to get what they want. It may work in the moment, but the change isn't long-lasting, which is one of the reasons why aggressive people repeatedly try to intimidate others.

The opposite end of the scale is being too passive and letting the other person walk all over you. While it may seem like being passive will make the problem go away, it actually keeps the problem alive. Nothing gets solved when things are one-sided; the tension is always hovering just beneath the surface.

When you're assertive, you stand up for your own rights without putting down others. It's the most effective way to solve problems. Here's the difference between aggressive, passive, and assertive behavior:

Aggressive = violating the rights of others

Passive = letting someone else violate your rights

Assertive = maintaining your rights while respecting the rights of others

Approaching your roommate assertively means confronting the situation instead of attacking the person.

How to Break the Ice

Confronting your roommate can be intimidating. Here's what you can say to hold your ground while bringing up an issue with your roommate:

1. "I respect your right to your opinions, but I see things differently. I want to talk about how we can work it out."
2. "It bothers me when the room gets this messy. We both have our own space, but when your stuff ends up all over the couch then it's affecting me too."
3. "I feel like my privacy has been invaded when I see that things on my desk have been moved."
4. "When the utility bill is paid late, it affects my credit. So I'd like to set up a payment schedule that would work for both of us."

5. "I'd like to talk to you about having friends over. I'm feeling crowded out of my own room. How can we work it out so that we both get some space?"

6. "I know we decided to share food, but it's not working out the way I thought it would. It would be better for me if we were to each do our own shopping."

The goal is to address the issue in a neutral manner without attacking the other person. By addressing the problem in an assertive manner, you're protecting your rights and probably heading off a major blow-up down the road.

My Roommate Is an Attack Dog

Even if you approach your roommate with the best of intentions, you may get attacked in return, especially if that's how she has responded in the past. People stick to what works. If you normally back down when things get heated, your roommate will turn it up immediately. Protect your turf—this may be your roommate's test to see how serious you are about the problem. If you can't be scared off, then she may calm down and deal. Let her know that you still want to talk, but you won't stand for verbal abuse or personal attacks. If the aggressive behavior continues, end the conversation by saying that you won't talk under these circumstances, and pick it up again after a cooling-off period.

Stay the Course

Whatever you do, don't get aggressive—that'll only escalate the situation. Your roommate will know that he's pushed your buttons and will keep pushing them. Here's how you can assertively hold down the fort when you're under attack:

1. "Please keep your comments focused on the issue rather than on personal attacks."
2. "This topic is important to me, but I won't continue if you insult me. Why don't we take a break?"
3. "This is getting too heated. Let's pick it up again after we've both had a chance to cool down."
4. "I want to talk to you, but not under these circumstances. When you're ready to work on the problem without yelling, I'm available."
5. "I want to solve the problem now but not if it means getting into a screaming match. Why don't we talk another time?"

Don't continue a discussion if your roommate refuses to stop yelling or becomes personally insulting. That type of behavior is a violation of boundaries. Walk away; go to a friend's room or to the library. Remember, we teach people how to treat us. Don't encourage aggressive behavior by staying around.

Just Say N-O to B.O.

"My roommate has decided he's going to save the environment by showering once a week. His B.O. is so bad the whole room reeks. I must have spent at least $25 on air freshener already. How do I tell him he smells?"

—JAMES, AGE 18

Got a roommate who needs a date with deodorant? Are rancid foot odors forcing you to dump shoes in the hallway? Does your roommate shed hair, drop fingernail clippings, pick-n-flick (boogars, that is), or publicly pop zits a little too often? Maybe you wanted to say something, but your roommate's breath is so bad you couldn't stand the conversation! Personal hygiene is one of those icky topics no one wants to bring up, but the best way to handle it is to be honest. When you're living in quarters small enough to qualify as a prison cell, you need to protect the air you breathe!

Save your roommate embarrassment by talking in private with no one else around. Be straightforward and respectful. There is a good chance he doesn't know there is a problem. There are a few other things to consider too. If your roommate isn't showering and appears overly tired to the point of not getting out of bed, he could be suffering from depression. Check out Chapter 11 for the complete list of symptoms and what to do. What you eat affects body odor, breath, and even hair loss, so maybe your roommate started a new diet and the results are less than pleasant. Finally, be sensitive to money issues. Some students are broke by the end of the month and may not be able to afford hygiene products that you'd never consider going without.

How to Break the Ice

Here's what you can say if your roommate's lack of hygiene is overwhelming:

1. "This is hard for me to talk about, but I need to tell you that your body odor is really strong."

2. "I'm sure you're not aware of this, and I'm not trying to embarrass you, but your breath doesn't smell so good. Are you on a new diet or something?"

3. "I need to talk to you about your shoes—the whole room is starting to smell like them. I think Odor-Eaters would take care of the problem."

4. "I know you like that perfume/cologne, and I like it too, but a little goes a long way. Can you cut down a little?"

5. "I noticed you haven't been showering for the last couple of days, and I wanted to make sure everything's okay."

Don't go on and on about how embarrassing this is for you to bring up. It will only make your roommate feel more uncomfortable. Instead, keep your comments straightforward and honest.

I've Offended My Roommate

What's worse, being offended or smelling offensive? If your roommate gets upset over your comments, it's probably because she is embarrassed. Offer reassurance that you didn't mean to cause hurt feelings, and then leave the topic alone for awhile.

It's Your Air, Too!

Here's what you can say if your roommate takes your comments the wrong way.

1. "I'm sorry if you feel embarrassed. I'm embarrassed too. I didn't know how to bring it up, but I was trying to be honest."

2. "I know it's embarrassing, that's why I brought it up in private."

3. "I won't mention it again, but I really felt I needed to say something."

4. "Maybe I didn't say it in the right way, but it was never my intention to embarrass you."

5. "Please understand that I don't want to hurt your feelings, but I needed to bring it up."

If your roommate's ego was bruised, it may take some time for him to recover before you see (or smell) a change. Give your roommate a little time and space to sort out any hurt feelings.

Tips to Remember

- You don't have to accept aggressive behavior. What people fear most about confrontation is not feeling prepared to handle the other person's reaction.

- Choose your battles, and weigh the pros and cons of bringing up a situation. Ignoring issues can have negative consequences, and speaking up can solve the problem and increase your self-confidence.

- The time to discuss how problems will be handled is when you and your roommate are getting along, not after issues have reached a crisis point.

- You don't need to be aggressive to confront your roommate. Be assertive, which means you stand up for your own rights while respecting your roommate's.

- If your roommate's lack of personal hygiene is grossing you out, be honest and respectful. Bring the issue up in private.

If you want to learn more about developing positive confrontation skills, visit your campus counseling center. Or check out the counseling Web site for the University of Illinois at Urbana-Champaign: *www.couns.uiuc.edu/Brochures/self.htm.* Find more courage by reading *The Coward's Guide to Conflict: Empowering Solutions for Those Who Would Rather Run Than Fight* (Sourcebooks Trade, 2003).

4

I'm Definitely *Not* the Problem!

Quick Quiz: True or False

If it weren't for my roommate's issues, everything would be fine.	T/F
Until my roommate changes, nothing can improve.	T/F
My RA needs to step in and do something about my roommate.	T/F

Score:

1 T: You feel like your roommate situation is out of your control.

2 Ts: Your four favorite words are: "This is so unfair!"

3 Ts: You no longer have bed sheets since you used yours to make a white flag.

Spinning out of Control

"I've never had a problem getting along with anybody until I met my roommate. She's a total drama queen and thinks the world revolves around her. I'm easygoing, so I end up just letting her ramble on since there's nothing I can do about it anyway."

—KARIN, AGE 19

It can be very challenging dealing with people who demand center stage. If you're not careful, you can get forced into playing a role yourself, that of the victim. In fact, overly demanding people need victims around them so they can feel like they're in control. If you're so frustrated that you've given up and assume that nothing can change because your roommate won't cooperate, you've slipped into a victim mentality.

You Might Be a Victim If . . .

Victims believe they have no power, control, or choices and thus feel helpless to change anything. They feel like situations (and bad roommates) are forced upon them and that there is absolutely nothing they can do to make things better. This ends up unintentionally forcing a negative outcome, because others really do start taking over when victims give up control. Check this list to see if you've adopted a victim mentality:

- You think the situation is hopeless and unfair.
- You're blaming others for what's happening to you.
- You focus on what others do *to* you instead of what you can do to change the situation.
- You're waiting for circumstances and other people to change before you do.
- You complain to others, but reject their suggestions.

If you recognize that you've been thinking like a victim, then you've already won half the battle! If you step back and take an honest look, you might see how you've contributed to the problem by allowing your roommate to take over. Now that you're aware, you can start turning things around by shifting your focus.

How to Break the Ice

While you can't control other people and circumstances, you always have control over your response to the situation. Here's how you can go from sounding like a victim to sounding like a person in charge of your outcome:

1. "I've been letting you make all the decisions, and I now realize that I need to be responsible for what happens to me."
2. "I'm not happy with how things are going, and I haven't done much to change that until now. I'm ready to be part of the solution, if you are."
3. "I've been blaming you for everything, and that's not fair. I'm willing to face up to my part and do what I can to make things better."
4. "Up until now I haven't said much, but now I'm ready to deal with the situation."
5. "I don't like the way things are, so I'm ready to focus on what I can do to change it."

If you're blaming your roommate for being 100 percent of the problem, then you're also making her responsible for 100 percent of the solution. Shift your thinking to what you can do, and let your roommate know that you're taking back control for what happens to you.

My Roommate Won't Give up the Reins

Don't be surprised if your roommate initially resists your efforts to even the playing field. He has been used to you folding, so it's confusing now that you're not. What happened to the old you? In order to get you to respond like you used to, your roommate will probably turn up the heat. Don't fall for it! You teach your roommate how to treat you by how you respond. If you go back to acting like a victim, your roommate will continue to treat you like one.

Don't Back Down!

Here's your chance to take back control. If your roommate is pushing you, stay the course and repeat your message. She will catch on soon enough. Here's how you can respond if your roommate is a slow learner:

1. "I know you're not used to seeing this side of me. I'm taking more responsibility for how things are, and that's not going to change."
2. "This situation is only going to work if I speak up, so I'm going to let you know how I feel from now on."
3. "I have a say in this situation and my own outcome."
4. "I used to think this problem was your fault, but that means there's nothing I can do about it, so I'm not going to think that way anymore."

Whenever you blame others you give them enormous power to make you happy or unhappy. Your roommate's controlling behavior may or may not change. Whatever happens, remember that only you control your attitude and how you respond.

Are You Insane?

> *"My roommate is disgusting! Her junk is everywhere. There are empty pizza boxes piled up next to dirty clothes. After she takes a shower, she drops her wet towel on the floor and leaves it. Every morning I clean up our room, and by the end of the day, it's right back where it started. She doesn't even thank me for picking up her stuff! You'd think she'd get the hint, but hello! We fight about it every day and nothing changes."*
>
> —JANICE, AGE 19

If you and your roommate are stuck in a rut of having the same fight every day, it can feel hopeless. You might think, "Why bother bringing this up again when I already know exactly what my roommate will say?" You're right! After awhile, it does no good to repeat yourself if it's not effective. Have you ever heard the definition of insanity? It's doing the same thing over and over again expecting a different result! You might as well skip the fight and hit the replay button. If you want a different answer, you've got to plug in a different equation.

You can break your current pattern of fighting by changing at least one thing. It doesn't have to be big and dramatic; something small can work just as well. You'll see a ripple effect. When you change, your roommate is forced to choose a different response, too. Sometimes it shakes things up enough to give you a fresh perspective.

Dig Your Way Out of an Argument Rut

Become aware of the way your fights usually go. What do you normally say? What tone of voice do you use? Where do you stand? Are other people present? When does the situation start going south? Once you know the pattern, start by changing one thing. Here are some examples of what you can do differently the next time you and your roommate have the same argument:

- If you always yell, stay silent.
- If you always keep your anger inside, say what's bothering you.
- If you always leave, stay in the room.
- If you always start by telling your roommate what she did wrong, start by listening.
- If you always use the same words to describe the problem, change them.
- If you always cross your arms while listening, relax them.
- If you always argue in the same spot, change locations.
- If you always fight at the same time of day, change times.
- If the TV is always on, turn it off.

The list is endless. The more you become aware of your own actions, the more control you have over the situation. You may think some of these changes are so insignificant they couldn't possibly make a difference. If so, refer back to the definition of insanity! Go ahead—change one thing. What have you got to lose?

Stop Pushing My Buttons

"My roommate thinks he has all the answers when it comes to girls and dating. He's always giving me advice, and if I don't follow what he says, he tries to make me feel guilty and stupid. I do my best to ignore him, but he really knows how to set me off."

—MIKE, AGE 20

How is it that some people know just what to say to get us mad or make us feel guilty? It's like they got the script from your parents! Actually, button pushers don't possess secret mind-reading powers, but what they do know how to do is gauge your responses. They watch and listen very carefully for what makes you feel guilty, mad, or intimidated. Once they've hit the target, they just keep repeating the same assault because it obviously works! Button pushers are all about control, but they can't be in control if you never show them where your control panel is located.

Hide Your Buttons

You could very well be inviting an attack by giving obvious signals to your roommate about what sets you off. Here are some phrases to avoid around a button pusher:

"You make me so mad!"

"Stop making me feel guilty!"

"Stop doing that, you know it upsets me!"

"You know I don't like it when you say that!"

"How am I supposed to feel now?"

"You keep saying that when you know it makes me feel mad/guilty!"

"Don't make me cry!"

If your roommate already knows your weaknesses and exploits them, you can still turn it around. Remember, nobody can make you feel a certain way without your permission. You're going to have to exercise some self-control not to react, but once you quit responding in an emotional way, your roommate will stop too. Try to remain calm and show no emotion, even if you feel like a robot.

How to Break the Ice

Here are some examples of what you can say if your roommate keeps trying to push your buttons:

1. "Let's focus on the issue and keep our emotions out of it."
2. "I'm not going to respond to that, but I will talk about the issue."
3. "I want to keep this conversation rational, so let's stick to the facts."
4. "I don't want to get off track, so let's keep focused on the problem."
5. "I've already shared my feelings about this. I only want to talk about how to solve the problem now."

Your roommate may try to get you off-balance by bringing up certain topics, using a tone of voice that makes you feel intimidated, or steering the conversation in the direction of feelings rather than facts. Don't fall for it! Don't discuss your feelings at that moment with your roommate. Protect yourself, and just talk about the facts of the situation at hand.

What If I Bug Out?

Telling yourself you're going to stay calm and then actually doing it in the moment are two different things. It's going to take some practice, especially if your roommate keeps pushing you. But it *is* possible to stop yourself before you totally lose it. First, there's no rule that you have to respond at all. If your roommate says something that hits you in the gut, you can remain silent. Who says you have to say something right away? Use that silence to *breathe*. It may sound funny, but when people get overly emotional, they often forget to breathe properly. They begin taking short, shallow breaths that lead to hyperventilation instead of deep, abdominal breaths. For more help, check out Chapter 14 for specific breathing exercises.

Take a Break

The first thing to do is to remember that you don't need to respond at all. You can take a break from the conversation as long as you agree to continue it later. Storming out of the room is another "gotcha" signal to your roommate. Here's how you can respond if you need some time to get your emotions under control:

1. "I'd like to continue this later tonight/after class/after studying."
2. "I feel like this conversation is getting off track, so let's take a break."
3. "I don't want to confuse the issue. Can we talk again in a little while?"
4. "I want to think this over, so how about we take a break?"
5. "I want to make sure I'm saying exactly what I mean. I need some time to think about this."

Don't let your roommate dictate the terms of your conversation. If you need a break, say so. Do something positive to get your mind off of the conversation if you find yourself getting emotional. Call a friend or get a change of scenery by going to the gym or even to the library. You have as much say in how the conversation goes as your roommate does.

Tips to Remember

- Beware of adopting a victim mentality. To get your power back, shift your focus to what you *can* do, instead of what's being done *to* you.

- While you don't have control over other people and circumstances, you always have control over your response to the situation.

- You teach others how to treat you by how you respond. Giving up control teaches your roommate to treat you like a victim.

- An argument rut is when you keep having the same fight and nothing changes. Break old patterns by becoming aware of how the argument usually goes and then changing one thing.

- Be aware what signals you may be giving that tell your roommate exactly how to commit emotional blackmail.

- Take a time out if you have trouble controlling your emotions. There's no rule that you must respond immediately.

You can learn more about staying in control by visiting your campus counseling center or checking out the information on managing emotions from the University of Texas at Dallas student counseling page: *www.utdallas.edu/student/slife/counseling/difficul.html*.

You may also want to read *Emotional Intelligence* by Daniel Goleman (Bantam, 1997).

5

Communication That Works

Quick Quiz: True or False

You use the silent treatment to get your message across. T/F

You won't talk to your roommate, but you complain
about her to other people.   T/F

You prefer writing notes and e-mails over talking to
your roommate in person.   T/F

Score:

1 T: You have only one response for your roommate: "Talk
to the hand!"

2 Ts: You wear headphones in the room even when you're
not listening to music.

3 Ts: You let your roommate know exactly what you're
thinking—with sign language.

Foot-in-Mouth Disease

*"My roommate is ultra-sensitive, and I don't always say things the right
way. She's constantly twisting what I say into something I didn't mean. I
try to explain, but it doesn't work. All we do is talk in circles."*

—ANGIE, AGE 18

Sound familiar? You know what you want to say, but it never comes out
right. Or, maybe you've experienced Foot-in-Butt disease—that's where
you kick yourself for saying something you later regret! When it comes
down to it, 99.9 percent of all roommate problems are due to lack of

communication. How can something most of us have been doing since the age of two be so difficult? Easy. Communicating well is a *skill* that needs to be practiced, and some people come to college more skilled at it than others. If you've never shared a room, dealt with confrontation, or problem-solved with someone you don't really like, then you may find it challenging to communicate in these situations. Throw in a little homesickness and stress over assignments and exams and suddenly the simple act of communicating can get really complicated.

The good news is that big changes can result from becoming aware of the subtle ways you may be sabotaging your message. By becoming a better communicator, you will be able to work things out with your roommate and immediately lower your stress level.

Yeah, But . . .

"My roommate is in love with his own voice and shares his opinions all the time. If I try to give my opinion, he cuts me off. He refuses to listen to anyone who doesn't agree or who doesn't make him look good. Now whenever he starts talking, I immediately tune out."

—ROGER, AGE 20

Without a doubt, the toughest part of fighting with someone is listening to her side when you think she's wrong. Listening well is the secret weapon to de-escalating an argument. It's more than waiting for the other person to stop talking so you can start or digging for ammunition. If you're really listening, you allow the other person to talk until you understand—and she feels understood. In fact, the real reason most people fight is not to get their way, but to be understood.

Empathic listening is listening with the intent of understanding. (Empathy is different from sympathy, which is feeling sorry for someone.) It means doing your best to stand in the other person's shoes to see the situation from her perspective.

Put Yourself in His Shoes

Understanding where your roommate is coming from does not mean you have to agree or share similar experiences. You don't even have to like the other person! But you do have to be able to step outside yourself for a moment and consider the other side. Here's what it takes to listen with empathy:

- Have a goal of understanding your roommate rather than defending yourself.
- Give your full attention; no multitasking while you listen.
- Concentrate on the message; don't think of your rebuttal.
- Paraphrase and clarify key points.

Remember, try first to understand, not to be understood. This can be hard if you're angry or you're discussing a sensitive issue, but it will de-escalate the argument and help you arrive at a solution.

Do You Hear What I'm Saying?

If you tend to tune out when your roommate starts talking, one of the best ways to stay focused and show you're listening is paraphrasing. That's when you repeat key points of the conversation back to the other person in order to clarify. Be careful not to do this by parroting each and every word, because that could be interpreted as teasing.

For example, if your roommate says, "I'm having a bad week, and I need space. When I come back to the room to find all your friends here, it stresses me out." To let your roommate know you understand, you might paraphrase back, "I get that you're stressed right now and want space to be alone."

How to Break the Ice

Here are some other ways to work paraphrasing into your conversation so that your roommate knows you're really listening:

1. "Let me make sure I understand what you're trying to tell me."
2. "This is what I hear you saying . . . "
3. "I'm not sure I understand what you mean. Do you mean . . . ?"
4. "So what you're saying is . . . "
5. "You want me to know . . . "
6. "If I've got it right, you feel . . . "

Paraphrase throughout the conversation so that you're clarifying as you go, rather than waiting until the very end to find out if you understood. The best time to do it is when there's a break in the conversation (your roommate has to breathe sometime!), after a major point has been made, and before you start to explain your side.

My Roommate Won't Listen to Me

Okay, you've done all this work to be a good listener, but your roommate is not returning the favor. Frustrating! Remember, listening is a skill, and not everyone does it well. Your roommate may need some help. By being a good listener, you encourage the same in others. Also, it helps to let your roommate talk first so that his feelings are fully vented and interruptions are less likely. Finally, come right out and describe what listening means to you. Complaining to your roommate by saying, "You're not listening to me," doesn't mean anything to a nonlistener. The response to that is usually a defensive, "Yes I am!" Before you begin speaking, set up your expectations by describing how you want to be treated.

Listening and Hearing

Ask your roommate to go for a walk or have a cup of coffee, since it may also help you both to have a change of scenery. Make sure to leave your cell phones behind to lessen the temptation for more distractions. Here's how you can encourage your roommate to hear and understand your side:

1. "Before I talk, I want to make sure that you've said everything you want to say and that you feel like I understand you. But I'd also like to be shown the same respect."

2. "It's important to me that you understand where I'm coming from, and it's easier for me to talk to you when you're not on the computer at the same time."

3. "I'm not sure if what I'm saying is coming across the right way, so can you let me know how you're interpreting it?"

4. "You might disagree with what I'm about to say; but, I'd appreciate it if you'd hear me out."

5. "I have something important to say, so I want to pick a good

time for you to be able to listen without other distractions. What time works for you?"

Be sure to give your roommate the chance to paraphrase you too. It does no good for you to keep talking if you notice a look of confusion or anger on the other person's face, because listening has stopped at that point.

Tongue Tied

"I know in my head what I want to say to my roommate, but when it comes time to speak I get flustered and then it doesn't come out right. It's like a brain freeze, and I can't think of the right words to explain how I feel."

—KELLY, AGE 19

Isn't it amazing how something can make such perfect sense inside your head, and then when you try to tell someone else it comes out a convoluted, jumbled mess? Moments like this tend to happen when emotions are running high, like when you're trying to tell your roommate that you're angry or hurt. If emotions trip you up, it's helpful to have a way to phrase things that works every time and includes everything you need to say. Here's a way you can be honest, specific, and take ownership for your feelings. Just fill in the blanks:

When _____(specific behavior or situation) happens, I feel _____ (what you are experiencing). What I need from you is _____ (what you want to happen).

If you can fill in all the blanks, then you're ready to have a conversation. It may also be helpful to practice a few times beforehand.

How to Break the Ice

Once you get the hang of communicating your feelings in this way, it will become more comfortable. Here are some examples of how to share what you're feeling:

1. "When I'm studying and the TV is blaring, I feel like there's no consideration for my rights. Could you keep the volume down?"

2. "Staying in touch with family and friends is important to me. It makes me angry when my phone messages get lost. Could you please write them down and put them where I can find them?"

3. "When your boyfriend is here 24/7, I feel like I have no privacy. I need us to agree that we won't have visitors at certain times."

4. "When your dirty dishes are left in the sink, it really bothers me. Can we agree that we'll each clean our dishes by the end of the day rather than leave them overnight?"

5. "When you refuse to talk to me for days, I feel hurt and confused. I need you to tell me how you're feeling."

6. "When I get interrupted, I feel like my opinions don't count. I need you to hear me out."

If you're still nervous about sharing how you feel, try writing it down first. Sometimes seeing things in black and white will help you understand exactly what's bothering you. Describing clearly how you feel in writing will help the words flow easier in conversation.

My Roommate Won't Open Up

Sometimes the key to opening up the floodgates is simply in how you ask the question. Avoid asking your roommate "why," as in, "Why did you do that?", because this immediately puts people on the defensive. Instead, use open-ended questions that require more information. Start with either "what" or "how," as in, "How do you feel about that?"

Leave Your Questions Wide Open

If your roommate only gives one-word replies, you may be asking closed questions where a simple yes or no is all that is required. Here's how you can respond with open-ended questions to encourage your roommate to talk more:

1. "What's going through your mind right now?"
2. "What happened to make you angry?"
3. "How do you want to solve the problem?"
4. "What changes do you think we should make?"
5. "Where do you think our communication broke down?"

The most important thing is for you and your roommate to work together to solve the problem. By asking open-ended questions, you'll get a better sense of the real issue.

You're "Shoulding" Me!

"My roommate talks to me like I'm twelve years old. He's so full of himself, it's annoying. He'll tell me what I can and can't do—like he's my parent or something! I don't think he even knows how he comes across."

—JEREMIAH, AGE 18

Little words can make a big difference in how you come across to others. How do you react when someone tells you what you *have* to do or what you *should* do? Sounds like your parents, right? The natural reaction is to rebel just to prove your independence. Another example of a word that changes the meaning of what you say is, "but," as in "I like you, but you drive me crazy." What part is true? The word "but" cancels everything that comes before it, so it sends a very confusing message. How about the word, "try" as in, "I'll try to be more considerate." There's a huge difference in the commitment level between *trying* and *doing*. If you merely say you'll try, you might notice others don't totally trust you to come through.

Words That Weaken Your Message

Do you find that people don't react to you the way you want them to, and you can't figure out why? It might be the difference of a few words. Here's a list of words to avoid:

Should, have to: These come across as condescending. Instead of telling people what they should do, offer suggestions. Then let them decide.

Always, never, everyone, nobody: These words rarely paint an accurate picture and come across as overdramatizing. You'll lose credibility. Instead, use words such as "sometimes," "occasionally," or "some people."

But: This negates everything that comes before it and can make you sound like you're talking out of both sides of your mouth. Replace it with "and," as in: "I want to be your roommate, *and* we have some issues to work out."

Try: This is one big escape clause and makes others question your commitment. Don't try, just do it.

You: Starting sentences like this comes across as attacking and blaming. Instead, be accountable by starting with "I."

Okay: Tagging this word onto the end of sentences makes it sound like you're asking permission: "I'm upset right now, okay?" Lose it, or people won't take you seriously.

These changes may seem small and subtle, but you'll be surprised what an impact they can have on how people respond to you. You may also start to notice that when you react negatively to someone, it's because she has used some of these phrases.

Mixed Signals

How you say something is even more important than what you say. The old phrase, "actions speak louder than words," really rings true. If you tell your roommate how much you want to work things out as you cross your arms in front of your chest and look at the floor or watch TV, the message you're sending is the exact opposite. A major sign that you're sending mixed signals is if people say to you, "I don't believe you," or "I don't trust you." If your verbal and nonverbal messages don't match, it is the nonverbal communication that will stick out in people's minds.

Become aware of what your body language is saying and whether it is consistent with your words. That includes eye contact (especially rolling your eyes), how you stand or sit, heavy sighs or head shaking while listening to something you don't agree with, and how much personal space you put between you and the other person.

Another nonverbal factor is your voice pitch, tone, and volume. Has anyone ever told you that "nothing" is wrong, but you know by their tone of voice there's a big problem? Remember, how you deliver your message counts more than what you say.

E-Fights

"Whenever my roommate is mad about something, I find out about it through an e-mail. It becomes total war, and we write things we'd never say to one another's face. It's so weird because we act like nothing's happening, while at the same time we're sending each other nasty messages. It causes even more hurt feelings since too many things get misinterpreted, and it takes twice as long to clear up."

—BARB, AGE 20

Have you been blindsided by an e-mail that you either think about for days or respond to immediately by firing back a nasty response, only to discover that you totally misinterpreted the meaning of the message? People who don't like confrontation love to e-mail, IM, or write notes! They are all convenient ways to avoid conversations that really need to be held face-to-face. A lot of courage must be locked up in those computer keys, since people often say things in e-mails that they'd never have the nerve to say in person.

The rules for using e-mail are simple: when the topic involves something emotional or requires any kind of feedback (good or bad), talk in person whenever possible. If you're sharing general information or planning where to meet, e-mail is fine.

You can waste a lot of time and emotional energy trying to decode the message behind the message or to guess whether someone's blog entries are about you. These are dangerous ways to communicate emotional information because they lack the benefit of nonverbal cues, tone of voice, and a chance to clarify in the moment. People end up responding to false assumptions and beginning a dialogue that's not based in truth.

As humans, we generally need eye contact and to hear the way something is said to help us understand. Words are just words; it's people that give them meaning. No happy or sad face icon can adequately describe how a person really feels.

How to Break the Ice

If your roommate tries to avoid tough conversations by e-mailing you instead of talking, don't engage. Instead, say in person that you received the message and that you'd like to talk about it face-to-face. Here's how you can let your roommate know you want to talk, not type:

1. "I got your e-mail, and there's a lot in there I want to ask you about. When is a good time to talk?"
2. "Thanks for your e-mail. I really want to talk to you about what you wrote. I'd feel more comfortable if we did it face-to-face."

3. "There are a few things in your e-mail that I'd rather talk to you about in person, so I can make sure I understand. Is now a good time to talk?"

4. "Rather than send e-mails back and forth, I think it would be quicker and easier to sit down and talk. When is a good time for you?"

5. "I got your e-mail and I'd like to respond. I'd feel a lot more comfortable doing that face-to-face though, so when is a good time for you?"

Technology comes in handy, but it should never be a total replacement for face-to-face communication, especially when strong emotions are involved. There's too much meaning that can get lost or misinterpreted.

Great, But I Can't Think on My Feet

That delete button comes in pretty handy when you're not sure what you want to say! With emotional topics, it is a good idea to think through what you want to say first and even practice the conversation. Many people use e-mail to vent or clear their thoughts. If you feel the need to do that, go ahead and write the e-mail. Just don't send it! If you can't imagine yourself facing your roommate and reading that message out loud, you know you're at the venting stage. There's nothing wrong with writing out what you want to say if that will help you clarify it. But don't fall into the avoidance trap; these conversations need to happen in person.

Use E-Mail to Set a Time

If you feel the need to start the dialogue with your roommate through an e-mail, send one that only asks that the two of you talk in person and that contains the issues you want to discuss. Here are some examples of what to say in your e-mail to encourage face-to-face dialogue:

1. "I need to talk to you about some things that are bugging me, and I want to do it when we both have time to sit down. Will you be around tonight?"
2. "I'd like to talk to you in person about having friends stay overnight. When is a good time?"
3. "I feel like there's tension between us, and I'd like to talk about it in person. What's your schedule like?"
4. "Will you be around to talk sometime today about our sleep and study schedules?"
5. "When can we get together to talk about how the phone bill/cleaning schedule/overnight guests should be handled?"

Notice that you're not inserting your feelings into the request for communication. Writing, "I need to talk to you about the overnight guest policy," would be fine. But adding a little nuance like, "I was really angry that you had your boyfriend sleep over the night before my big exam," might set your roommate off. Keep the e-mail neutral, and talk about your feelings in person.

Tips to Remember

- The majority of all roommate problems are due to lack of communication. It's a skill that needs to be practiced.

- Listening with empathy is the most effective way to de-escalate an argument. You don't have to like, agree with, or have shared similar experiences with the person to have empathy.

- Avoid asking "why" questions as they put others on the defense. Open-ended questions require more than one-word responses and encourage dialogue.

- Actions speak louder than words. If your body language is inconsistent with your words, the nonverbal message is the one that will stick.

- Don't use e-mail as a substitute for speaking about issues face-to-face. Use e-mail to share facts or details, such as a place and time to meet, but talk about your feelings in person.

You can test your communication style at Southern Illinois University Carbondale's counseling Web site at *www.siu.edu/offices/counsel/talk.htm*. You might also want to check out *Tongue Fu: How to Deflect, Disarm, and Defuse Any Verbal Conflict* (St. Martin's Press, 1997).

6

Odd Couple:
Personality Differences

Quick Quiz: True or False

You have nothing in common with your roommate.	T/F
You and your roommate are like night and day.	T/F
You and your roommate can't agree on anything.	T/F

Score:

1 T: Your roommate gets on your nerves, but you're dealing with it.

2 Ts: Sucks to be you. You're doing everything you can to avoid your roommate.

3 Ts: You spend your free time sticking pins into voodoo dolls that closely resemble your roommate.

Sorry, You're Not My Type

"My roommate and I disagree on everything, even the type of beer we like. I have afternoon classes, and he has morning. He gets up at the crack of dawn and flips on all the lights. He calls me lazy because I like to sleep in. I like sports, and he's into computers. He gets on me about how I eat, dress, and study, like he's my parent! I can't make a move without him telling me I'm doing it wrong. I feel like I have to brace myself for an attack every day."

—ADAM, AGE 20

Are you living with your total opposite? It's amazing how different two people sharing the same (tiny) room can be. Even the littlest things can drive us crazy after awhile! You eat Big Macs and chicken wings while your roommate swears by tofu and beans; you like Coldplay and your roommate cranks up Tim McGraw. You're East Coast; your roommate is West Coast. Whatever your differences (and there are bound to be a few), you need to figure out what you're willing to live with and what's fair to ask your roommate to change.

Your roommate may have an accent that grates on your nerves, but that's not something you can ask a person to change. It's also not fair to expect someone to change her entire personality to suit you. It would be great if we could snap our fingers, and BAM, instant personality makeover! Not gonna happen. So, you need to separate his personality from his irritating habits. You won't transform your roommate into your new best friend, but you can make things a lot more bearable.

Polar Personalities

Think about how you describe yourself: Confident? Quiet? Determined? Easygoing? Would you rather party or study? Do you like to plan things in advance, or are you the last-minute type? Everybody has her own style that has taken her years to develop. (Your roommate has worked her whole life to become such a pain!) We behave in ways that fit our personality and make us comfortable. While it's not reasonable to ask people to change who they are, you can ask them to tone down how they express themselves, especially when it's invading your turf.

Let's say your roommate is really outgoing and talks nonstop. You can't ask him to suddenly become quiet and subdued, but you can ask for no conversations first thing in the morning or when you're studying. Maybe you're living with someone who's a neat freak and constantly rides you about your dirty dishes. Okay, let her be neat, but establish a reasonable timeline in which to do dishes before you hear about it. Your roommate could be thinking two minutes, and you're thinking twenty-four hours. Keep the conversation focused on what's negotiable rather than on personality types.

How to Break the Ice

Focusing on your roommate's personality rather than her habits or behavior can come off like an attack. Defenses will go up and positive communication will come to a screeching halt. Here are some ways to approach your roommate about toning down irritating traits without being offensive:

1. "You've probably noticed I'm not as talkative as you. It's not that I mind conversations, but I can't talk first thing in the morning until I really wake up."

2. "I'm willing to clean my dishes. It just may not be as soon as you do yours. Can we compromise?"

3. "I can tell you're spontaneous, but I'm more of a planner. When it comes to having parties in the room, can we talk about how I can have some advance warning?"

4. "It's cool that we're different. I don't want to change that. I just want to figure out a time when it can be quiet in the room so I can study."

5. "We definitely have different tastes in music. I'm not asking for you not to play yours, but I want to be able to play my stuff too. What can we do when we're both in the room at the same time?"

6. "You have a lot of friends on campus who want to hang in our room. When I'm done with classes, I like to chill by myself. Is it possible to not have any visitors at least for an hour?"

Habits and behaviors can be hard to change. Just think of how comfortable you are with your own habits. Don't expect your roommate to do a complete overhaul all at once. Change comes in a matter of degrees.

My Roommate Is Attacking My Personality

Personality traits are neither right nor wrong, neither good nor bad—that doesn't prevent people from making judgments. It's an impossible battle to fight, because you end up trying to justify your right to be you. That doesn't mean you don't have any annoying habits. Keep the focus of the conversation on what you can do to become more compatible with your roommate, not what's wrong with your personality.

Help Me Help You

Not everyone knows how to give feedback. If your roommate majors in personal attacks rather than offering something you can change, here's how you can respond:

1. "I'm not willing to change who I am, but I will do what I can to get along."
2. "What exactly are you asking me to do differently?"
3. "If we're going to work this out, we need to focus on things we can change."

4. "I'm not asking you to change your personality. I'd appreciate the same respect."

5. "I like who I am, and I'm not going to change my personality. But I will consider adjusting some of my habits so we can get along."

By re-directing attacks on your personality to habits and behaviors that can be changed, you'll soon teach your roommate your limits. Repeatedly defending your personality will only invite more attacks.

Ten Things I Hate About My Roommate

"My roommate has long, black hair. It ends up everywhere. It clogs the drain. It's all over the floor and couch. I even found it on my clothes, which grosses me out the most. Not only that, she insists on watching the stupidest TV game shows, and she snorts when she laughs. Everything that she does gets on my nerves."

—RANDI, AGE 18

We all have our pet peeves. Maybe facing an empty toilet paper roll every morning is enough to drive you over the edge. For someone else, it could be missing phone messages. Know yourself. What can you absolutely not deal with? What do you find extremely irritating, but could live with if you had to? There are probably tons of things your roommate does that get on your nerves. But nothing kills a relationship faster than listing dozens of reasons why you don't like a person. When things are tense, it's best for each person to start with one request for change.

Make a list for yourself of all the things your roommate does that make you want to yank your hair out. Then go through each one and decide whether it's a deal breaker or just really annoying. In some cases, it may be a matter of degrees. Take your list of really annoying habits and set it aside. You'll have to live with those for now. Narrow your list of deal breakers down to your number one pet peeve. If you're having trouble choosing just one, ask yourself which thing would dramatically improve your relationship if it changed tomorrow. That's the place to start. Make sure it's something your roommate has the power to change, like not blasting the radio when you're trying to study or not borrowing your clothes without asking. Describe a specific behavior or incident rather than, "You need to be more fun."Ask your roommate to do the same thing and pick something she'd like to see changed.

How to Break the Ice

Telling someone about his irritating habits can be a touchy subject, to say the least. Remember to stick to just one pet peeve. Asking someone to completely change all her habits would be overwhelming and likely to provoke a negative response. Here are some ways to approach your roommate:

1. "It's obvious we think differently about a lot of things. But I think we can make this work if we both agree to change one thing."
2. "We're both miserable with how things are. So what if we concentrate on making changes in one area, and see how that goes?"

3. "We can't change everything overnight. What if we each concentrate on changing one thing?"

4. "Let's start small. Tell me one thing you want changed, and then I'll tell you one thing I'd like to see changed."

5. "We all have our pet peeves. Chances are I'm doing things that drive you nuts. Why don't we each discuss our number-one issue?"

One habit may seem like a drop in the bucket when you're at your wit's end. Don't despair. If you and your roommate can successfully compromise on just one thing to start, you will have built a foundation of trust to work on other issues in the future.

Annoying Habits Galore

When we're talking about pet peeves, it's easy to get on a roll and let everything fly. That is especially true if resentments have been simmering for awhile. When you're getting hit, the temptation is to strike back with your own long list of complaints. Neither one of you is really listening at that point, so the situation is not likely to improve. But it's good that you're talking, so to keep that going, when it's your turn to talk, calmly explain that you're willing to start with one issue. Don't bother defending or discussing the rest.

Stop the Snowballing

It's much better to go slowly and address one or two things at a time in a conflict situation. If your roommate hits you with an endless list, here's how you can respond:

1. "I want to work with you, but I can't change everything at once. Why don't you tell me your number one pet peeve, and we'll go from there."

2. "I can only focus on one thing at a time. Can you narrow it down?"

3. "This much feedback at once is overwhelming. How about we address one pet peeve at a time?"

4. "I'm getting hit with too much. Let's start with one thing, and see how it goes."

If your roommate still has trouble focusing on just one pet peeve, you can help narrow the focus by bringing up something you'd be willing to address. Saying something like, "I heard you mention that you don't like my clothes on the floor," can help keep the conversation positive and moving forward.

Take a Number, Please

Opposite personality types tend to have a tough time reading one another. It's actually possible for your roommate to have no clue that she's bothering you. Your roommate may not be able to pick up your subtle (or not so subtle) hints, especially if you're the type to keep things inside. You can say, "That really bugs me," over and over again, but it all sounds the same after awhile. Your roommate may interpret "bugs me" to mean "no big deal." Meanwhile, you're ready to blow! That's why it's helpful to use a scale of one through ten. Think of it as volume control.

Here's how it works. Pick a time when things are calm, and talk to your roommate about your number-one pet peeve. Give examples of when you felt things were out of control and say, "For me, that's a ten." Then give an example of what you consider a halfway, revving-up point and call that a five. Choose a milder example, and call that a two. Ask your roommate to give you the same kind of examples. By using numbers, both of you know where you stand.

How to Break the Ice

Using a numbers system is like having your own private short-hand. It also lets your roommate know how much things bother you without confusing the issues with too much emotion. Here are some ways you can begin speaking the same language as your roommate:

1. "I don't think you understand how much this upsets me. If I were going to put a number on it, this is a ten."
2. "Give me an example of when you consider everything to be fine between us, something you would rate as a one or two."
3. "I'm not always mad. Right now, I'm cool with how it's going with us. On a scale of one to ten, I'm at a two."
4. "I can't always tell when you're really pissed off and when you're okay. On a scale of one to ten, what are you right now?"

This is a good way for you to notice whether you tend to wait for things to get to a ten before speaking up. Obviously, the sooner issues are addressed the easier they are to resolve. So if you notice you're starting to get angry in silence, don't wait to say something.

My Roommate Lives at Ten

All-or-nothing types have a hard time knowing when to scale back. Your roommate may be so upset right now that she can't focus on anything less than a ten. However, being mad 24/7 is emotionally and physically exhausting. If your roommate wants to live in a drama, that's fine. Just don't offer to share the rent.

Take It Down a Notch

If your roommate is stuck at ten, here are ways you can respond:

1. "I understand that you feel things deeply, and I respect that. But when you go from zero to ten over one thing it's overwhelming for me."
2. "There must have been a time when you weren't as angry about this situation as you are now. When was it?"
3. "Things weren't always this way between us. When did you think it was better?"
4. "Tell me when you think things between us went bad. What happened before that?"
5. "I have a hard time knowing when I'm setting you off. How can I tell, so I can avoid escalating the situation?"

By using a numbers system, your roommate gets to express his level of frustration, anger, or any emotion in a way that's clear and safe. It is an effective tool for neutralizing the situation before it gets out of control.

Can Opposites Attract?

Before you decide that life would be better with a roommate exactly like you, think of what you could gain by living with your opposite. We're often attracted to people who are different from us because they represent qualities we wish we possessed. If you're shy, maybe being around a more outgoing person will force you out of your shell. When one person's strength makes up for the other's weakness, being opposites is an advantage. Having opposite schedules, for instance, can be a good thing when you're fighting for bathroom time.

There isn't just one right way to do things. If your roommate makes different choices than you would, that's all that her choices are—different. They're not good or bad, so be careful about judging other people's choices. What works for you may not work for them and vice versa, and that's okay. Another thing to consider is that this is prepping you for the real world. You don't get to choose your boss or coworkers on the job. (Granted, you won't have to live with them.) If you can learn to live with someone who is different from you, you can probably work with anybody!

Sign on the Dotted Line

A lot of colleges require roommates to sign formal contracts. Even if you don't take it that far, it's a good idea to get your differences out in the open. If you never had a discussion with your roommate about the basics, it's a way to get a fresh start. You might even discover that you agree on a few things. A little common ground is better than nothing.

If you actually do write up a contract, make sure it's something both of you create, rather than a list of your demands. Also, decide what will happen if one of you breaks the agreement. A contract is useless if there are no negative consequences. So put that part in writing, too. If your roommate offered to share his stereo equipment with you, and you break the contract, a negative consequence could be that you lose stereo rights. Sometimes contracts are written up at the beginning of the semester before you really know your roommate. Then two weeks in, you wish you could change the rules. Items in the contract could be re-negotiated and changed at any point as long as you both agree on them. Establish a time period to check in with one another to make sure things are still working. It could be once a month or every couple of weeks. After you both sign it, make copies for one another, one to post, and one for your RA. Being accountable to someone else tends to hold people to their word. Here are some topics you'll want to discuss:

Guests

- When is it okay to have guests over?
- How much advance warning is needed?
- Will one roommate with a guest have exclusive rights to the room? If so, for how long? Where will the other roommate go during this time?
- What happens if a guest damages property?
- What if both of you want to have guests at the same time?
- Are there different rules for same sex vs. opposite sex visitors?

Personal Property

- What's okay to share? What's off limits?
- What happens if something is touched without permission?

Cleanliness

- What's your idea of clean? What do you consider messy?
- What's necessary to keep your space livable? Whose responsibility is it?
- Where does dirty laundry go?
- How should the bathroom be kept? Kitchen? Bedroom? Common area?

Study/Quiet Time

- What are your hours of study?
- Is it okay for your roommate to watch TV or listen to the radio while you study?
- Is it okay for your roommate to work on the computer while you sleep?
- When do you sleep/get up?
- Are there different rules for the weekend?

Telephone/Mail

- Where do you want your phone messages and mail to go?
- How will the phone bill be handled?
- Do you want to "cover" for one another (tell callers you're not there when you are)?
- Is there a time limit on how long one person can be on the phone?
- Is it okay for your roommate to talk on the phone when you are sleeping or studying?
- Are there certain hours when friends should not call?

Shared Costs

- Should you split costs on anything? If so, how will bills get paid (cash, check, credit card)?
- If you split food or laundry products, how do you decide what's fair?

Smoking/Drinking

- Will smoking and/or drinking be allowed in your room? If so, under what conditions?
- Is anyone allergic to smoke?

Personal Space

- How will your room be decorated?
- Are there any areas that should be off limits?
- What happens if someone puts up something offensive?

Disagreements

- How will you handle disagreements?
- How will you handle updates to your contract?
- What if someone breaks the contract?

Other Issues

- Is there anything else you need to know about each other to get along?
- What's the most important thing you each want respected?

Discussing all these issues up-front prevents a lot of future hassles. You may think it's too much work or that you'll be able to deal with problems as they arise, but it's much harder once emotions cloud the issue. Just like nobody gets married expecting to divorce, nobody enters a roommate situation expecting to not get along. Still, it happens. It's worth it to have some guidelines in place.

Tips to Remember

- It's not fair to ask someone to change his or her personality, but you can ask for it to be toned down around you.
- Focus on what a person can reasonably change.
- Separate your real pet peeves from annoying habits you can learn to tolerate.
- Choose only one pet peeve to address at a time instead of several. Allow your roommate to do the same.
- Use a scale of one to ten to help your roommate understand where you're coming from and when the situation is getting out of control.

You can learn more about personality types by visiting your campus counseling center and requesting to take the Myers-Briggs Personality Type Indicator or you can take the test online at *www.discoveryourpersonality.com*.

7

They're All Against Me:
When Roommates Gang Up

> ### Quick Quiz: True or False
>
> When your roommates talk, it's like you're not even
> in the room.   T/F
>
> Your roommates make major decisions when you're
> not there.   T/F
>
> You hear about your roommates' weekend plans
> after the fact.   T/F
>
> *Score:*
>
> 1 T: You're convinced you're being filmed for an MTV
>   reality show.
> 2 Ts: You're wondering if OutKast needs a new member.
> 3 Ts: You've been voted off the island.

It's Freezing in Here

*"Freshman year I lived in a quad with three other girls who were friends
in high school. It was three against one from the start. They excluded me
from everything. I tried to talk with them, but they had their own inside
jokes. Anytime I'd ask what was going on they'd say, 'Nothing.' After
awhile, I gave up."*

—MICHELLE, AGE 21

It's bad enough getting the cold shoulder from one roommate, but when
it's a group, it can feel downright cruel. It's natural for people with similar personalities and interests to hook up. Cliques can form right away

or over time. Opposite schedules can also cause you to be left out of the loop. Even if you're living with your best friends, relationships can change once you're forced to share the same space. And the more roommates you have, the harder it is to get everyone on the same page.

Remember, you don't have to like or agree with every person you live with, just respect them. Each group of roommates has certain dynamics, just like your family has its own quirks. One person's drama can affect the whole group. The trick to fitting in is knowing when to stay quiet and ride it out and when to speak up.

Stages and Rages

There is some level of conflict in *every* group of people who live together, whether they know each other or not. Why is this? Every group goes through the same five stages: *forming, storming, norming, performing,* and *adjourning.* Some groups click right from the start and progress quickly. Others get stuck. Some groups do fine until they hit a bump, and then they end up back at the beginning. You may want to avoid the "storming" or conflict stage because it makes you uncomfortable. But if stages are skipped, your group will never gel. See if you can recognize what stage you and your roommates are in right now.

The Five Stages of a Group

It's the goal of every group to gel and get along. But, notice that in order to do that, the group will go through a conflict stage:

1. *Forming.* This is when you first get together. People are slightly nervous, and their guards are up. You're checking

each other out, forming impressions, and wondering if you'll fit in.

2. *Storming.* Personalities start to emerge. There's jockeying for turf. Someone claims a certain bed; someone else announces a shower schedule. Leaders step up, and followers fall in line. You learn that people have different ideas about how to do things or treat one another. This is when conflicts arise. Roommates who constantly argue can get stuck here.

3. *Norming.* Game rules are established. Sometimes they're formal, like in a roommate contract. Many times they're unspoken. You learn by observing that it's okay to swear around one roommate and that another is always late with the rent. If you're stuck in a bad situation, it could mean that the norms include unhealthy rules like gossip or backstabbing.

4. *Performing.* This stage is the goal. Your roommates are in a groove. Everyone does her own thing, and each person feels respected.

5. *Adjourning.* Saying goodbye. It can either be positive, neutral, or nasty.

There's no timeline for these stages. You and your roommates could move through them quickly, or it could take all semester. If your group seems to be stuck and is not moving forward, try going back to the previous stage and working on it.

I'm Not Acting Paranoid, Am I?

When are you being too sensitive, and when should you say something? That's the dilemma of the person who is the third (or fourth) wheel in a roommate situation. How can you be sure your roommates are purposely trying to squeeze you out? What if you've misread the situation? We tend to assume the worst about what others think of us. The more bad feelings exist the more we go on hyperalert. Every little exchange comes across as a personal attack, even if it was never intended that way.

The only explanation you can come up with for why your roommates acted a certain way is that they hate you. That could be true, but it's only one possibility. Every story has more than one side to it, but when you're feeling paranoid, you think it's all about you. Force yourself to consider all the other possible explanations before you assume the worst. Rather than jumping to conclusions, gather the facts.

Let's say your roommates went to the movies without inviting you. How many reasons can you come up with to explain what happened? Of course you can't know for sure until you talk to them. But the way you first react to the situation makes a big difference. Shift your thinking to a more objective perspective.

Paging Sherlock Holmes . . .

You need to think more like a detective than a judge to try to figure out the motivations for your roommates' behavior. A judge makes a final decision. A detective gathers evidence, talks to everyone involved, and comes up with a hunch. How might a detective approach what could have happened when your roommates didn't invite you to the movies? Here are some possibilities: Maybe they couldn't find you. Or they thought you already saw the movie. Or the car was full. Or it wasn't their idea; someone else invited them. Or it was a spontaneous decision and they didn't think to invite you. Or they thought you didn't have the money. Or maybe, they just don't like you—but before you reach that conclusion you can probably think of a bunch of other reasons why you weren't invited. Using a detective mindset opens up a whole range of possibilities, only the last of which is the worst-case scenario that they don't like you.

Just the Facts, Ma'am

What's the evidence for your assumptions? What exactly did your roommates do or say that made you decide they don't like you? People are innocent until proven guilty. When you approach your roommates, base it on more than a gut feeling that they're out to get you.

How to Break the Ice

If you accuse someone of being a snob or acting like a jerk with nothing to back it up, you'll be out in the cold. Here are some ways you can approach your roommates in an open, fact-finding way without coming off as paranoid:

1. "I heard you guys went to the movies. Could I join you the next time?"
2. "I noticed when I walked into the room, you stopped talking. Did I interrupt a private conversation?"
3. "I saw you roll your eyes when I asked to join you for dinner. I'm not sure what that means. Can you fill me in? "

4. "Lately it seems like whenever I come into the room, you leave. Is something wrong?"
5. "When I left the room, I heard all of you laughing. What'd I miss?"

Watch your roommates' responses. Sometimes when a group of people have been tight for awhile, they don't realize that their actions come off as hurtful or exclusionary. The reality check may be that you'll never fully be part of the group if your roommates are close friends, but at the very least they may gain some understanding of how their behavior comes across.

My Roommates Are Pretending Nothing's Wrong

Passive-aggressive behavior is when a person attacks you behind your back, but won't confront you to your face. The best way to respond is to focus only on behavior—what a person does or says. Stick to the facts. Sometimes just calling out someone's behavior is enough to make it stop. Whatever you do, don't accuse anyone of lying. Most people won't admit to lying, but will lie more to cover up, creating an endless, frustrating loop.

Denial Ain't Just a River . . .

If your roommates tell you that nothing is wrong, then take them at their word, but use it as an opportunity to gather more information. You don't have to call them liars to stand your ground. If you see things differently, say it without attacking them. Here are some ways you can respond to denials:

1. "I'm glad nothing's wrong. I'm just wondering though, if there was a problem, how would you let me know?"

2. "I just wanted to make sure I wasn't reading the situation wrong. When you guys leave as soon as I come home, it feels like I'm being excluded. How do you see it?"

3. "Obviously, we have a different take on the situation. When you guys make plans right in front of me, and don't invite me, it makes me feel left out or that you're angry with me."

4. "I'm glad to hear you say that nothing's wrong, though I don't know what to think when I see you rolling your eyes."

5. "I'm glad to hear there's no problem on your end. For me, it's kind of weird to have you all stop talking when I walk into the room."

6. "What you call 'nothing' still bothers me. Being left out of inside jokes makes me feel excluded. Since you said they're no big deal, can I be let in on a few?"

Your roommates may still insist nothing is wrong, but at least they'll know how their actions are coming across to you. Also, they can't tell you that you're just "imagining things" when you are able give specific examples of behavior.

Pssst, Did You Hear About . . .

"My roommates gossip all the time. Especially one girl. All she does is put down everyone else when they're not there. I'm sick of hearing it. She even spread a rumor that a girl was pregnant when she wasn't. I worry she talks behind my back, too."

—Vanessa, 18

Gossip is a form of passive-aggressive behavior. The same people who feel safe talking behind your back rarely have the guts to say it to your face. There's only one way to handle gossip: don't do it. If you listen to gossip, even if you don't add to it, you're sending the message that it's okay. You're guilty by association. Plus, if you hang out with people who gossip, you can bet they're talking about you too.

How to Break the Ice

Communication should always be directed to the person involved in the situation. Don't make someone else's issue your business. It will always backfire. Here's what to say when a roommate starts talking to you about someone else:

1. "Talking to me won't change anything. Why not tell her to her face?"
2. "It doesn't do any good to tell me this. Talk to him."
3. "I don't like talking about people behind their back."
4. "I don't want to get involved. Let's talk about something else."
5. "This isn't my business, so I don't even want to hear about it."
6. "Sounds like you need to tell it to her, not me."

It's easy to get sucked into gossip. Oftentimes it feels like a way to build camaraderie or to be part of a group. The peer pressure to gossip can be intense. However, it's more than likely that at some point the tables will turn and the joke will be on you if you join in.

What if My Roommates Gossip about Me?

If you find out through the grapevine that your roommates are talking behind your back, you have one of two choices. The first is to ignore it entirely. Don't fuel the fire. If it's not true, why defend yourself? The second is to address it once and only once. If you put energy into chasing down gossip and clarifying it more than once, you validate it. You lower yourself to the level of the person gossiping. If your roommates continue to backstab, you're not going to change them. Don't waste your time.

If you decide to say something, be direct and firm. Make your point, and be done. Be prepared if the gossiper tries to throw you off track by shifting the conversation to finding out who told you the gossip. A gossiper wants to make it all about naming names and attacking the source. Don't get sucked in. Say something like, "What I care about right now is hearing from you whether or not you've been trashing me behind my back." If your roommate says no, but you suspect the answer is yes, you can still make your point. (Remember to resist the urge to call someone a liar.) A strong response is, "Good. I'm glad to hear you say to my face that you don't gossip, because I don't tolerate it. Apparently you handle things like I do. If you have something to say, you go right to the person involved."

Keep Calling Her Out on It!

Calling the gossiper's bluff may be enough to shut her down. If not, here are some other ways to respond:

1. "I've heard you've been saying things behind my back. Let's talk about it face-to-face and clear the air."

2. "I'm confused why you'd say something behind my back that you wouldn't say to my face. Here's your opportunity. What do you want to say?"

3. "Your gossiping hurts me a lot, especially since I would never treat you that way. Either say what you have to say to my face, or don't say anything."

4. "When you talk about me to other people, I don't have the chance to respond or change anything. So what don't you want me to hear?"

5. "I don't tolerate gossip. Next time, say what you have to say to me, not everyone else."

6. "I understand you've been talking behind my back. I'd like to get everyone together and get the story straight once and for all."

Remember that gossiping is a passive-aggressive behavior. Whether the gossip will stop completely depends largely on the group dynamics of your roommates and peers, but oftentimes you'll find that gossipers don't have nearly as much to say if they know that sooner or later they'll have to explain it to your face.

Desperately Seeking Someone

One way to take the pressure off your living situation is to beef up your social life. If you're relying solely on your roommates for entertainment, then you can come across as too desperate. Ask yourself, "If these people weren't my roommates, would I choose to hang out with them?" If not, then it's time to go your own way.

Come up with a list of things you like to do when you're alone so you'll always have something to fall back on. Getting ditched doesn't feel half as bad when you have other things to do! Rent a movie, splurge on a dinner out, exercise, listen to music, read for fun, or find a new hobby! Work on developing at least two new friendships. Search campus bulletin boards for groups to join that interest you. Strike up a conversation with someone in your class, and ask if she wants to study together. Talk to your RA, who may know people with interests similar to yours. Hang out in social hubs like the campus coffee shop, join a church, or socialize with people at work. The more you develop a life outside of your roommates, the less you'll care about them.

We Already Decided

"My roommates always waited until I was gone to make major decisions. Once I came home to find out we had a fifth roommate—some guy I didn't even know. When I complained, they said they already took a vote and agreed, so it didn't matter what I thought anyway."

—ERIC, AGE 21

It sucks when majority rules, and you're never in the majority. Once decisions have been made, it's hard to backtrack. Focus on the future instead. If you're being excluded, it's important to speak up and let your roommates know you want a vote. Every time you stay silent, they'll assume it's okay to do things without you. Pick a time when no decisions have to be made, and establish ground rules. Make the topic "next time" instead of rehashing history so that you won't come off as defensive or attacking.

How to Break the Ice

When you're in a group living situation, most of the time you have to compromise with what the majority wants. However, it's not much of a democracy if your thoughts/feelings/ideas are never given equal time. Here are some ways to ask that your opinions be considered:

1. "I'd like to have a say in what happens. Next time, can we set up a system that involves everyone?"

2. "Next time a major decision comes up, I want to be included. How are we going to make sure everyone gets a vote?"

3. "I think it's only fair that everyone's opinion gets heard. Next time, what should we do if our schedules conflict and people aren't here?"

4. "Since I pay rent too, my opinion counts. How about we set some ground rules for next time?"

5. "There's bound to be other situations where we need to make a decision together. I want to be involved next time."

6. "Next time, if a decision needs to be made and I'm not here, can you wait at least 24 hours?"

Standing up for your rights will make it harder for your roommates to ignore you. Since they're not coming to you, it's important that you bring up the topic.

Wait, I Live Here Too!

If your roommates ignore your requests to be included on major decisions, stay cool. As much as you may want to blow up, it won't solve anything. Assume the detective role again, and find out the facts. What happened? Make your request again, but this time, make it more detailed and specific. Create a simple agreement together that everyone signs (see Chapter 6 for more ideas on roommate contracts). Spell out exactly the type of decisions you want to be in on like bills, rent, utilities, furniture, hosting parties, or any decision you really care about.

Second Time's a Charm

If your roommates still cut you out of decisions that affect you, that's reason enough to consider moving. Here's how you can respond if your first request has been ignored:

1. "Based on what we discussed last time, I thought we agreed you'd talk to me before you made another big decision that affects me."
2. "I thought we had an agreement. What's up?"
3. "There still seems to be a misunderstanding about what I want a vote on. Adding cable is an example of something I care about because I will have to share the expense of it."
4. "I don't understand why you guys made this decision and didn't ask me about it."
5. "I'd like all of us to sit down together and put the house rules in writing so there won't be any more misunderstandings."

If your roommates continue to exclude you from decisions you might have to take more assertive action such as not paying your part of the rent. If you pay, you are entitled to a say. Be careful with this though! This is a last-ditch effort that could escalate the conflict and damage your credit rating. If it gets to this point, then it's probably time to move out and move on. Talk to your campus housing service about alternative arrangements.

Getting Back on the Team

If you and your roommates have had a blowout, the tension can be unbearable. Loyalties split with people taking sides or with nobody talking at all. Although it's certainly not your job to get everyone talking, it usually takes one person stepping up to the plate if anything is going to change. You might need to be the bigger person in this situation.

How to Break the Ice

Your making an attempt to get back on track doesn't guarantee cooperation. The worst that can happen is that they refuse to talk, in which case you're no worse off than when you started. At least you'll know you tried. Here's how you can start off the conversation:

1. "I don't know about you, but I don't want to spend the rest of the semester not talking. What's it going to take to fix this?"
2. "I said some stuff I regret. Maybe other people did too. Can we start over?"
3. "I know we're all angry. I'm willing to drop this, if you are."
4. "Living with this tension is no fun. I'm sorry if I offended anyone. Can we call a truce?"
5. "If I offended or upset you, I'm sorry. I'm willing to hear you out and start over."
6. "What if we agree to make certain topics off limits?"

Don't be discouraged if at first your roommates, as a group, don't respond positively. There's a tendency for people to stick with the pack in public just to be safe. You may find later that individuals will approach you one-on-one, in private. All it takes is one person to meet you halfway to break the deadlock.

To Each His Own

If your roommates want to hold a grudge, let it go. It's nothing you can fix or control. Sometimes people just need space to breathe. All you can do is make yourself available and send the message that you're open to a fresh start. Avoid telling your roommates you know how they feel, because you don't. You may have experienced the same falling out, but each person has his own perception of what happened. Don't assume you know anyone else's story.

Leave the Windows and Doors Open

Here's how you can respond and leave the situation open for future communication:

1. "I understand you have your own point of view. Let me know if you ever want to talk about it."
2. "This whole thing has caused a lot of hurt feelings. I hope we can work it out."
3. "If you don't want to talk now, I'll be around later."
4. "I'm open to talking about this when you're ready."
5. "I know you want some time. I'm going to back off, but just know I'm following your lead."

You can't force someone to forget a grudge; it's an individual decision. Holding a grudge gives people a sense of power, so they tend not to give it up just because you said something. They want you to know things are better because *they* decided it was over. Once you open the door, give it some time, and let your roommates approach you.

Tips to Remember

- All groups go through five stages: forming, storming, norming, performing, and adjourning. Give your roommates a chance to move through all of them.
- Don't make assumptions about your roommates' behavior or feelings. Gather all the facts before you approach them. Every story has more than one side.
- If someone talks behind your back, either ignore it or address it firmly one time. Listening to gossip only encourages it.
- Develop outside social interests and friendships. The less you rely on your roommates, the less desperate you'll appear—and feel.
- If important decisions are being made without you, speak up and let your roommates know that you have a right to participate.
- Someone needs to be the first to break the ice after a blowup. Just because you want to work it out doesn't mean everyone else will. Let them know you respect their feelings, and keep your door open.

If you're feeling isolated, check out *www.campusblues.com*. A good book to read is *Emotional Blackmail: When the People in Your Life Use Fear, Obligation, and Guilt to Manipulate You* (Quill, 1998).

8

Culture Clash

Quick Quiz: True or False

You barely understand a word your roommate says.   T/F

You needed a map to see where your roommate
is from.   T/F

You've never heard of most of the food your
roommate likes.   T/F

Score:

1 T: You're kicking yourself for not paying more attention
in your foreign language classes.

2 Ts: The term "cultural divide" has new meaning for you.

3 Ts: You're now working at the GAP in order to save
money for a single room.

Culture Shock

*"I thought it would be fun to room with a foreign exchange student. But my
roommate hardly speaks English, and I don't speak his language either.
He doesn't get half of what I'm saying, and he's serious all the time. We
don't have anything in common."*

—JARED, AGE 20

If you ask yourself who you're most comfortable being around, it's usually someone similar to yourself. If you have a group of diverse friends,
there's still some common thread that ties you together—even if it's
just enjoying the fact that everyone is so different. Cultural differences

can be challenging to understand and accept when another person's experiences are so different from your own. Language barriers are obvious, but there's much more. Our culture teaches us what we perceive to be "normal." It helps define how we think, behave, and communicate. Culture guides our choices in food, music, clothes, and friends. If your only exposure to different cultures has been eating your way through the mall's international food court, then you're in for a crash course! For example, in American culture, it's taught that using direct eye contact and smiling at someone is a positive way to communicate. But, in Asian culture, direct eye contact can be interpreted as challenging the other person, and constant smiling can mean that you're nervous or revealing too much emotion. Each culture interprets the other's behavior as being rude! Misunderstandings like these can easily lead to roommate conflicts. Culture shock is a real thing, and you don't have to be from another country to experience it. Any group that shares certain values and expectations has its own culture. If you belong to a fraternity or sorority, you know exactly how you're supposed to act in order to fit in. The culture of the South is much different from that of the East. Farming communities have a different culture than communities of the inner city. Some students experience culture shock when they first get to college from high school; it's not just the people who are different, it's the whole environment. Culture shock can make you feel completely out of sorts, like you don't belong anywhere.

If you or your roommate is experiencing culture shock, it can certainly put a strain on the relationship, especially if you're not familiar with it by name. Some signs of culture shock include: feeling angry over minor inconveniences, irritability, withdrawal from people who are different from you, extreme homesickness, and sudden intense feelings of loyalty to your own culture. Others experience their discomfort physically by having stomachaches, crying, or feeling a need to sleep excessively.

What's important to remember about cultural differences is that there is no right or wrong. We only know what we grew up with, and that seems normal to us. This varies depending on race, gender, ethnicity, socioeconomic status, geography, and even the individual.

How to Break the Ice

The best way to bridge the gap between cultures is to learn more about your roommate as a person. You can't make assumptions about a person or generalize her background. Here are some ways you can ask about a culture that's different from your own:

1. "Tell me more about how you grew up."
2. "What holidays does your family recognize? How do you celebrate them?"
3. "What was it like growing up in your family? What did you do for fun?"
4. "What's the biggest difference between this culture and the one you grew up in?"
5. "How would you compare your country/hometown to being here?"

While most people appreciate sincere interest and a desire to understand where they're coming from, they may not want to discuss certain aspects of their culture. Certain topics such as religion or politics can be very charged for people. Be respectful. Follow your roommate's cues, and don't pursue any topics he seems reluctant to talk about.

Oops, I Offended My Roommate!

You can have the best intentions in the world, and still end up offending someone. Depending on the tone of your voice, questions can come off as judgmental or sarcastic. Your roommate may be overly sensitive if she already feels like a cultural outsider. If you spout off twenty questions in a row, it'll feel more like an interrogation than a friendly conversation. One way to build trust is for you to offer up something about yourself first, and then ask a question. You can't expect a person to reveal more than you would yourself.

I'm Sorry (in Any Culture)

We all have different limits on what we consider to be too private or personal, so your roommate may be suspicious about your motives. Share a little bit of information at a time to test the waters. If you overstep your bounds, apologize and take it as a sign to move more slowly. Here are ways you can respond if you unintentionally insult your roommate:

1. "I'm sorry. I had no idea you would find that offensive. I won't do it again."
2. "I apologize. Where I come from, that's no big deal. I didn't think it would bother you."
3. "I don't know a lot about your culture. I didn't mean to be insensitive."

4. "In my culture, that's not considered rude. I'm sorry if I offended you. Can you let me know what's off limits?"

It may take some time to figure out how to avoid misunderstandings and culture clashes with your roommate. Just respect your roommate's differences, and keep the lines of communication open.

Don't Stand So Close to Me

"The guy I live with stands way too close to me. He's a loud talker to begin with, but then he stands about two inches from my face. It's like he wants me to fight or something. Finally I told him to back off, and he had no idea what I was talking about. He didn't think there was a problem."

—MIKE, AGE 21

If you like your personal space, you may not enjoy your roommate standing so close that you can smell what he had for lunch! If you're on the quiet side, you may be shocked at how loud your roommate talks. If you look a person in the eye when you speak, you may be offended if your roommate refuses to make eye contact as often or as long. What you may not know is that all of these situations are examples of how culture affects our communication styles. A couple of misinterpretations can lead to major misunderstandings, especially when neither person thinks she is doing anything wrong!

Different Strokes for Different Folks

While it's important not to stereotype individuals, there are some broad communication differences according to Derald Wing Sue and

David Sue, who are noted authors in the field of cultural diversity. See if you recognize yourself in the descriptions below. How do you fit in or differ? What about your roommate?

Personal Space

In the United States, we tend to become uncomfortable if someone we don't know well stands too close or touches us. Anywhere between four and twelve feet of distance is considered acceptable. But in other countries like South America, Africa, and parts of Europe, people may feel comfortable standing much closer while talking.

Smiling

Western culture associates smiling with being friendly, positive, confident, intelligent, and having a good personality. But in some Asian cultures, smiling can be associated with embarrassment, discomfort, and shyness. Among some Japanese and Chinese people, outward displays of emotions are discouraged.

Shaking Hands

Shaking right hands seems to be universal. But, in some countries even touching another person with your left hand is of the highest insult. Some Muslim and Asian cultures view the left hand as dirty.

Eye Contact

In American society, using direct eye contact shows interest, respect, and self-confidence. But in some Asian and Native American cultures, using direct eye contact is considered disrespectful and challenging, especially if the other person is an authority figure.

Silence

Americans are not comfortable with long pauses in conversation and tend to take it as a signal as their turn to talk. However, silence is not necessarily a sign for others to pick up the conversation for many Chinese and Japanese. It may mean just the opposite; the person intends to continue speaking. In traditional Asian cultures, being silent in the presence of one's elders is respectful. Native Americans also traditionally equate silence with respect.

Volume

Americans and Europeans tend to speak loudly compared to people of Asian descent, who speak more softly. American visitors to Asian countries are often viewed as aggressive in their speech and body language.

That's What I'm Talking About

Just because you and your roommate have different communication styles doesn't mean you can't get along. Most of what we learn about communication is unconscious; we picked it up as kids and give it little thought. You can ease the tension by becoming more aware of your own style and by talking about differences.

How to Break the Ice

Approach the conversation with an attitude of sincere interest in wanting to learn more. As long as you're open to feedback, you'll put your roommate at ease. Here are ways you can begin to speak the same language:

1. "I want to understand you better, but since we communicate differently, I think I sometimes get the wrong message."

2. "Compared to you, I feel like I talk loudly. But sometimes, I can barely hear you. Do you notice the difference too?"

3. "It's a little uncomfortable for me when you stand so close. Our cultures define personal space differently."

4. "Our backgrounds are different and so are our communication styles. Sometimes I have trouble understanding what you mean."

Building a relationship and understanding your roommate's communication style can take some work, but it will be worth it. Cultural differences aside, all human beings have the need to be validated, understood, and respected.

My Roommate Won't Talk to Me

If trying to clear up communication differences makes your roommate clam up, don't jump to conclusions. It doesn't necessarily mean he is mad. Remember, silence can have several different meanings depending on a person's culture. Show respect and try being silent, too. Wait and see what happens instead of filling the space with mindless chatter.

Another possibility is that your roommate took your comments the wrong way and feels too embarrassed or self-conscious to speak. Sometimes building trust takes longer for some than for others. Maybe your roommate is not ready to start talking about personal styles. It may take the whole semester to learn how to communicate with one another, so give the situation some time.

Let's Try This Again . . .

Here's how you can respond if earlier conversations backfired:

1. "I'm not sure what your silence means, but I'd really like your feedback. Is there some way I could improve the communication between us?"
2. "Thanks for listening. I'm ready to hear you out whenever you feel like it."
3. "I'd really like to know what you think. If you don't want to talk now, that's cool. I'm open to discussing this any time you're ready."
4. "I'm having trouble reading your reaction to what I said. Could you give me some feedback? I care about your thoughts/feelings."
5. "I hope you feel comfortable enough with me to talk about this. If not now, maybe later."

Once you've said this much, stay silent. You can't say you'll listen and then do all the talking. Allow your roommate the chance to respond. If nothing happens, at least you know that your message was heard.

Politically Incorrect

"I can't say anything around my roommate without setting off an argument. She twists everything I say into an insult about her race. I swear I'm not prejudiced! But if I tell her that she says I must be, otherwise I wouldn't need to defend myself. I can't win with her."

—JILL, AGE 19

Are you walking on eggshells around your roommate, afraid of saying something that's not politically correct? If you make an observation about differences in looks, language, beliefs, politics, family, religion—anything—does that mean you're prejudiced? Knowing the right way to phrase something can be tricky. What's okay with one person may not be acceptable to another. And as societal awareness grows and changes, so do the words and phrases that are considered okay to use. It's easy to slip up!

The label of prejudice (prejudging) is a heavy label with a lot of negative associations. You can't be expected to know and understand everything your roommate considers to be offensive. Everyone has the right to her personal beliefs, even if those beliefs are considered prejudiced by some. But there has to be a balance of opinion and respect if you're going to get along with your roommate.

How to Speak Without Offending

Even though the rules for what's PC and what's not often change, here are some general guidelines to consider before you share your views:

Avoid using all-inclusive language. Words like, "always," "never," "all," and "everyone," are rarely accurate descriptions. Instead, use words like, "usually," "sometimes," and "some people."

Respect the individual. No matter what you believe about a certain culture, base your comments on the person standing in front of you.

Allow for differences. Your views are neither right nor wrong—they're just different than your roommate's.

Speak for yourself. Own what you say or believe by starting your conversations with "I." When you start with "you," it comes off as attacking the other person or labeling.

Listen. Before you speak, listen and observe how your roommate talks. Using the same type of references is probably pretty safe.

When in doubt, ask. If you're not sure how to phrase something around your roommate, just ask. It's the ultimate sign of respect.

These are good guidelines to keep in mind when communicating with anyone. The most classic bit of advice—think before you speak—will also help you remain sensitive to others.

How to Break the Ice

If you've been accused of being prejudiced or stereotyping, it may feel like anything you say could be potentially explosive. Here are some ways you can approach a conversation when you're not sure what's safe to say or how to say it:

1. "I'm not always the most politically correct person, but that doesn't mean I'm trying to be insensitive."

2. "Just because I don't agree with everything you think doesn't mean I'm prejudiced. It just means we have different views."

3. "I don't want to get into a battle of labels. We're both individuals, and that's how I want to relate to you."

4. "My views are based on my own experiences. I know your experiences are different. That doesn't make either one of us wrong."

5. "I'm not trying to be rude, but I don't know how to refer to your race/culture. What do you prefer?"
6. "I respect what you're saying. I hope you'll offer the same respect to me."

We each have our own way of defining respect. You can't go wrong by asking your roommate how he defines it, then adjusting your communication style accordingly.

My Roommate Is Prejudiced

If the tables are turned, and your roommate is making unfair or offensive remarks, it can be just as uncomfortable. You may feel it's important to try to enlighten your roommate's views. Perhaps it's just a case of him not having enough experience to know any better. Your roommate may be receptive to another viewpoint as long as you keep the tone respectful and educational rather than taking on a condescending tone. Not many people are willing to sit through a lecture about how ignorant you think they are!

Maybe your roommate refuses to consider your views, which can make you feel even more frustrated. While you can't control other people, you can let your roommate know what you find offensive. Yes, everyone has a right to her opinion, but that doesn't equal free reign to walk all over your beliefs.

She Doesn't Quite Get It . . .

Don't bring up the issues that you already know you and your roommate don't see eye-to-eye on. Learn to choose your battles.

Here's how you can respond if your roommate is making culturally offensive remarks:

1. "When you make those comments, I feel like you don't have a full understanding of who I am and what my culture is about. I'm willing to tell you more if you're willing to listen."

2. "I'm not sure you're aware that I find your comments offensive. We both have a right to our opinions, and even though I don't agree with yours, I respect your rights. Please respect mine."

3. "We have opposite points of view, and we're both passionate about them. It's probably best that we agree to disagree."

4. "I feel put down when I hear those remarks about my culture. Maybe you're not aware how important it is to me, but I'm willing to talk more about it."

5. "I feel your impressions about me and my culture are off-base, and I'm hurt by some of things you say. I'm willing to talk more about it so we can understand each other better."

6. "I'm willing to hear your viewpoints, if you'll agree to listen to mine."

You can't educate someone who doesn't want to be educated, but you will have opened the door by offering to share more about yourself. Even if your roommate isn't willing to change her views immediately, that doesn't mean you haven't made a positive impact.

Tips to Remember

- Different cultures have different ways of communicating. Subtle differences can be misinterpreted.

- If your roommate won't talk to you, it's not necessarily a bad thing. For some cultures, silence is a sign of respect.

- Culturally sensitive conversations offer respect for the individual, allow for differences, and include accountability for your personal views.

- Deal with a roommate who is prejudiced by sharing what you find offensive and offering to provide more information. If your roommate refuses to listen or change opinions, agree to disagree.

You can learn more about adjusting to cultural differences by visiting your campus counseling center. The University of Wisconsin-Eau Claire's counseling Web site also offers excellent information on culture shock at *www.uwec.edu/counsel*.

9

What If My Roommate Is Gay? (Or, What If I'm Gay and My Roommate Is Straight?)

Quick Quiz: True or False

You have a feeling your roommate is gay, but
you're too embarrassed to ask.   T/F

You're fine with having a gay roommate; it's your
parents and/or friends that are uncomfortable.   T/F

Homophobic messages have been left on your
door about you and/or your roommate.   T/F

Score:

1 T: You've adopted the military's policy of "Don't Ask,
       Don't Tell."

2 Ts: You're watching reruns of *Will & Grace* for tips on how
       everybody can get along.

3 Ts: You've finally figured out the meaning of all those
       LAMBDA posters around campus.

Straight Scoop on Being Lesbian, Gay, Bisexual, or Transgender

*"When I found out my roommate was gay, I was scared he was checking
me out. I had never been around gay people before. We talked about it, and
it turned out he was cool, but it took me awhile to get used to the idea."*

—JOHN, AGE 22

Finding out your roommate is gay can bring lots of questions to mind:
Will my roommate be attracted to me? Will she try to convert me?

What if my roommate sees me naked? Will other people think I'm gay just because my roommate is? If I think my roommate is cute, does it mean I'm gay or bisexual?

If you don't have friends who are gay (that you know of), it may feel overwhelming to suddenly be rooming with a gay student. Whatever questions you have, they need to be answered if you're going to feel comfortable with the situation. Sexual orientation is just one part of a person's identity, and you don't have to like or agree with everything about your roommate in order to get along.

College tends to be a time of sexual experimentation. It's a time when you start to learn more about who you are. Some students feel freer to express themselves once they're away from home. In some cases, it may be the first time a person feels safe enough to come out as a lesbian, gay, bisexual (attracted to both sexes), or transgender (a person who is born one sex, but feels like the opposite). It can be scary, confusing, and exciting all at the same time.

In general, campus environments are tolerant of sexual exploration. If someone experiments sexually with another person of the same sex, it doesn't necessarily mean that the person is gay. Some people briefly engage in flings or relationships with the same sex, and then decide it's not for them, while others confirm feelings they've had for awhile.

If you're nervous about your roommate's sexual orientation, talk about it! The best way to face a fear is to get more information. He'll let you know if you're getting too personal. Most likely, you'll find that your roommate will appreciate the opportunity to be open and honest.

How to Break the Ice

Discussing sexual orientation can be an embarrassing and emotionally charged topic. If you've never known someone who is gay, bisexual, or transgender, you may be afraid of offending your roommate or of just sounding stupid. Here's how you can start a conversation on what can sometimes be a sensitive topic:

1. "Since I've never had a roommate who is gay, I'm not sure what to expect. I'd feel more comfortable if we could talk about it."

2. "I've never had a gay friend. Would it bother you to talk about it?"

3. "I've heard a lot of rumors about gay people . Can we talk about what's true and what's not?"

4. "The only gay people I've seen are on TV shows, but I don't know how much of that stuff is real."

5. "I've never known anyone who is gay. Would you be willing to talk about it with me?"

Respect your roommate's right to privacy. For some students, college can be a time of freedom to express and explore feelings they've had for years. For others, the process of discovering their sexual orientation can be confusing and traumatic. If your roommate is unable or unwilling to talk about it, your RA or college counseling service is also a good resource.

What If I'm Morally Opposed?

College presents you with a lot of challenging ideas, people, and situations. You won't agree with all of them. No one can tell you how to think or feel about homosexuality, and it may be an issue that you're unable to see past. However, it's not fair to view a person only in terms of their sexual orientation. How would you feel if your entire identity were reduced to being heterosexual? Take away sexual orientation, and your roommate is just another student who is going to class, eating pizza, begging for gas money, and hoping to land a good job some day.

No matter who you live with, you need to discuss your feelings regarding sex in the room, when friends come over, and whether sleepovers are okay. If it bothers you to see your roommate being intimate, agree on the times you'll be out of the room and vice versa. If you know for a fact that your visiting parents won't be able to handle the situation, make arrangements to accommodate schedules. Everything's negotiable as long as it's done with respect.

You Don't Have to Agree with It, but You Gotta Accept It

Here's how you can stick to your beliefs without offending your roommate:

1. "It makes me uncomfortable to be in the room when you and your partner are together. What if we come up with a schedule that works for both of us?"
2. "I understand where you're coming from, but my parents won't. I wanted to give you advance warning so you can decide if you want to be in the room when they're visiting."

3. "No matter who I roomed with, I'd feel uncomfortable with sleepovers. Can we work out a plan?"

4. "I have strong beliefs on this topic, but we don't have to agree on everything to room together."

5. "We have different viewpoints on this issue. It would be better to talk about the ways that we're similar."

6. "I don't think either one of us in going to change our minds, so let's agree to disagree."

College is about preparing yourself for the real world. You may find that as you get to know people who have different lifestyles/ideas/beliefs than your own that some of your feelings may change—or not. Don't feel pressured to change your beliefs just because others want you to. Respect their choices, but ask them to respect yours as well.

Dealing with Harassment

"My roommate is a lesbian. We get along fine, but I'm starting to get teased by other people who assume I'm her girlfriend. People leave nasty notes on our door and make rude comments when I walk by."

—GRACE, AGE 20

People can be mean. Depending on the level of tolerance on your campus, your roommate may be getting hassled over her sexual orientation. You might become a target too, just because you're sharing a room. Whatever the situation, sexual harassment is not okay. Nobody should have to experience it or endure it.

Check your college's sexual harassment policy to see how it's defined and the proper procedures for dealing with it. Since every state is different, each college has its own guidelines. Not every policy includes protection from harassment due to sexual orientation or for being *perceived* as gay, but many do. Some policies leave a lot of gray area that is open to interpretation. In the broadest terms, sexual harassment can involve the behavior of either gender against a person of the opposite sex or same gender. Here is a general definition of sexual harassment:

- Repeated, unwelcome comments, gestures, or touching of a sexual nature
- Repeated behavior of a sexual nature that has the purpose or effect of interfering with an individual's performance, as a student, or otherwise
- Behavior that creates a hostile, offensive, or intimidating environment
- A request for sexual favors that impacts the individual's academic or work experience

This list is certainly not all-inclusive. The most important thing is to listen to your instincts. If a fellow student or faculty member is doing or saying something that feels like harassment, chances are it *is* harassment. If you are truly in doubt, talk to your RA or go to your campus counseling center.

Should I Speak Up or Ignore It?

People who get bullied or harassed are often told: just ignore it, and it will go away. No way! Unless harassment is exposed, it will continue. In fact, silence promotes intolerance. People who harass others thrive on their victim's feelings of weakness, defenselessness, and helplessness. The more you feed into that, the more you enable the other person's sense of control. It's important to speak up, but in a way that's safe for you and that does not invite more abuse.

First and foremost, consider your personal safety. If it's a situation where you feel you could be harmed, do not engage by sharing dialogue. Leave immediately, and report the incident to campus police, your RA, or the counseling center. In addition, file a report according to school policy and the designated officer or department. Document dates and times and gather evidence: names (if you know them), examples, pictures, phone messages, and e-mails.

Speak up Against Harassment

If you choose to respond verbally, do so in a way that shows you're in control. If you lose it emotionally, argue, or fight back, your harasser will gain just as much as if you stayed silent. Her total goal is fear and intimidation. In order to combat that, you need to look that person in the eye and speak in a calm, confident tone of voice. Here are some ideas on how to keep it simple but firm:

1. "I find your comments offensive, and they need to stop."
2. "I don't like what you're saying to me. Knock it off!"
3. "Your jokes and gestures aren't funny. Please don't do it in front of me again."

4. "I'm not okay with the way you're talking to me. Your behavior is inappropriate."
5. "I won't accept any more comments like that."

Focus only on the behavior you want stopped without using generalities like "You're putting me down," or "You're harassing me." Make it brief, direct, and don't get sucked into analyzing the other person's motivation.

What If the Other Person Threatens Me?

Take threats seriously! Being threatened is part of what creates a hostile, intimidating environment. It doesn't matter if they're never acted on; the threat alone warrants reporting it. Do not attempt to reason with a person who makes threats. His goal is to create fear in you. He could care less about hearing another point of view. Don't try to confirm whether or not the comment was intended as a threat by asking, "Is that a threat?" What counts is how it makes you feel.

People who make threats are skilled at steering people off-track, usually by saying something like, "Can't you take a joke?" Don't take the bait. In this case, the only response is to report the incident immediately.

I Have Something to Tell You

"I want to tell my roommate I'm gay just because I don't want to hide anything. I've dropped a few hints to see how he'd react and if he'd say anything negative. He seems like he's pretty open-minded, but still I'm nervous."

—JAY, AGE 18

For gay or bisexual people, coming out is a process of understanding, accepting, and valuing one's sexual identity. If, when, how, and to whom you come out are completely your decisions to make. What works for someone else may not be the answer for you. So there's no expectation that you need to share this aspect of yourself with your roommate. But you may feel comfortable being open, especially since college living puts you in such unusually close conditions that it's hard to keep anything private.

In some ways, telling your roommate may be easier because she doesn't share a history with you and has no preconceived notions of who you are. You get to be in control of the information you share and the image you project. If you're thinking about coming out to your roommate, here are a few things to consider:

- Make sure you're comfortable with your own sexuality. If you're struggling with questions, this may be too vulnerable of a time for you to share or discuss your sexuality with your roommate.
- Think about the timing of your conversation. Pick a time when there will be no interruptions and your roommate is not dealing with other stuff.
- Think about what you want to say and how to answer questions your roommate may have. Consider rehearsing the conversation ahead of time with a campus counselor or RA.
- Be prepared in case the initial reaction is negative. Your roommate might respond with silence or shock and may need time to process what you've just shared.
- Have a support system in place like a friend, support group, or counselor to whom you can turn in case things don't go well.

- Be careful not to let your self-esteem depend entirely on the approval of others. If your roommate rejects you, that's not your fault.

Coming out is a process. Keep building your support system so that no matter what, you always know that you have a safety net of people who love and care about you.

How to Break the Ice

If you decide to come out to your roommate, make sure it's a good time to talk for both of you, a time when there won't be interruptions. Here are some ways you can open up the conversation:

1. "I have something private to share that I think is important for you to know if we're going to room together."
2. "I want to be totally open and honest with you. I'm gay. I realize you may be uncomfortable with that, so I wanted to have a conversation about it."
3. "You may or may not know that I'm gay. If you want to talk about it, I'm willing to answer questions so that we both feel okay with rooming together."
4. "I want you to know that I'm gay. If you need some time to process that, I understand. We can either talk now or later."
5. "I wanted to tell you that I'm gay. For me, it doesn't affect us rooming together, but I'm not sure how you feel about it."
6. "It's important to me that you know I'm gay. If you feel that's going to make a difference in how we operate as roommates, then we can talk about it."

Your own comfort level will set the tone for the conversation. The more at ease and factual you are, the easier it will be for your roommate. Make it clear that while you're not seeking your roommate's approval, you are sensitive to the fact that she might be uncomfortable.

What If My Roommate Rejects Me?

Keep in mind that your roommate's initial reaction may be more surprise than rejection. Given time, initial shock can turn to acceptance. Be patient and allow enough space and time to process the information. If it turns out your roommate chooses to have a negative attitude, it in no way invalidates your self-worth. It does mean that you may have to re-evaluate your relationship and your expectations.

We'll Talk Later

Here's how you can respond if your roommate reacts negatively to your sexual orientation:

1. "Everyone reacts differently. Let's give this some time and see how it works out."
2. "If you're not ready to talk now, we can talk later."
3. "Maybe this needs some time to sink in. How about we talk again later?"
4. "It would be a lot easier if you could accept this, but if you can't, it's still possible to be roommates."
5. "I can understand if you feel surprised by this and want more time to process it."

6. "It seems like you feel uneasy right now, but then again you haven't had a chance to really think about it. What if we give it some time?"

Tips to Remember

- Sexual orientation is just one part of a person's identity. You don't have to agree with it to be able to get along.
- If you're uncomfortable, talk with your roommate. The best way to face fear is to find out more information.
- Sexual harassment can affect you and/or your roommate. Ignoring it will not make it go away! When addressing a harasser, consider your personal safety and remain calm, brief, and direct.
- If you're gay, whether or not to come out to your roommate is a completely personal decision. Before you do, make sure you are comfortable with your own sexuality and have a support system in place.

You can learn more about sexual identity by calling the Gay and Lesbian National Hotline at 1-888-843-4564. Their Web site is *www. glnb.org*. For a Web site that specifically addresses gay issues on a college campus, check out *www.campuspride.net*. If you are gay and in a Greek system, visit *www.lambda10.org*. To learn more about the legal rights of gay students, contact the Lambda Legal and Education Defense Fund at *www. lambdalegal.org*. Finally, if you are gay and struggling with coming out, you can find support in others' personal stories at *www.comingoutstories.com*.

10

Three's a Crowd

Quick Quiz: True or False

You spend more nights sleeping in the lounge than
in your room.   T/F

You have to step over people to get to the bathroom.   T/F

When you get out of the shower to dry off, you
realize your towel has already been used.   T/F

Score:

1 T: You're getting straight A's since you spend a lot of
      time in the library.

2 Ts: You consider the extra people as part of the décor.

3 Ts: Your roommate's significant other is receiving mail at
      your address.

Friends Without Benefits

*"My roommate would put a bandanna on our doorknob to let me know
that he was 'busy' and that I had to bunk in someone else's room for the
night. He would even use a different color for certain individuals. The
problem was never really solved. I just asked him to not 'be busy' as much
in our room and to take it somewhere else."*

—ROB, 20

Are you finding out that sharing a room with your roommate also
means sharing it with boyfriends, girlfriends, or assorted one-night
stands? If you're lucky, you get some advance warning. If not, you

probably know what it's like waking up to the sounds of people having sex in a bed two feet away from you. Accommodating your roommate's sexual exploits can get old fast (especially if you're single). It's also one of the toughest issues to handle. University housing has clear and usually strict policies regarding overnight guests. But that doesn't mean rules don't get broken! And that's what makes this a delicate issue since busting your roommate could mean that you get in trouble too. In fact, the reality is that few students choose to speak up on this topic. That doesn't make it right, but it does make for overwhelming peer pressure to stay quiet.

If you're stuck in this position, it's important to talk to your roommate because you have rights too. It doesn't have to be an issue of staying overnight; maybe it's just that her boyfriend is omnipresent and crowding your space. You should definitely not be the one who has to leave the room all the time. If you do, your roommate will assume nothing is wrong, and the problem will persist.

Choose a time to speak to your roommate when the two of you can be alone. Explain that you have nothing against the boyfriend involved, but you feel uncomfortable having him around all the time. It's unreasonable to dictate to your roommate when and where she can carry on with her romantic life, but you do have a say when it affects your time in the room. Make sure you speak directly to your roommate, not the boyfriend, since the two of you are ultimately accountable for what happens in your room.

If you happen to be single at the moment, some people may try to use that against you by saying, "If you were dating someone you'd understand," or "You're just jealous." Even if you were dating someone, you'd still have to work out the issue of sharing the room. So don't fall for the guilt trip. Another pressure tactic is when your roommate says, "Where else are we supposed to go?" That's not your responsibility. Don't feel that you have to leave unless you can provide a list of alternative make-out areas. Don't worry—if they're desperate, they'll come up with something!

How to Break the Ice

Here are some ideas for how you can approach your roommate about romantic visits and overnight stays:

1. "I understand you want to be with your girlfriend. I'm just asking to have some advance notice so we can figure out what's convenient for both of us."

2. "I don't want to leave the room every time your boyfriend comes over, but I'm willing to be flexible. What do you think is fair?"

3. "I feel like your girlfriend is here a lot, and sometimes I just want to be alone to relax. Could we agree on some times when we have no visitors?"

4. "It's hard for me to study when your boyfriend is here so much, and I don't think it's fair that I have to go to the library every time. Is it possible to designate guest-free times so we can study or quietly relax?"

5. "It's not that I don't like your girlfriend, it's that I feel crowded out of my own room. So can we talk about what would work for both of us?"

6. "What if we split having the room to ourselves every other weekend so neither one of us feels completely put out?"

Bring up the topic of overnight guests when you and your room-mate have the time and space to discuss it—not while their significant other is in the shower. Your roommate may be truly oblivious to the fact that his having sex in the next bunk bed really bothers you. People can be very self-centered when love—or hormones—take over. If this is your roommate's first girlfriend, be understanding about his feelings, but firm about your right to not be kicked out of your own room.

My Roommate Brings Home Strangers—Every Weekend

Not everyone makes the best decisions when it comes to hooking up, especially when alcohol is involved. If your roommate is bringing home strangers who make you uncomfortable, you absolutely have to speak up. Not doing so could put your safety in jeopardy. Another issue is privacy. If something of yours should get broken or stolen, would you be able to track down the one-night stand? This is not an opportunity to lecture your roommate, but instead to share your feelings and set clear boundaries for yourself.

Hello, Do I Know You?

Have the conversation at a time when you're both alone and calm. Here's how you can respond if your roommate appears to have a revolving bedroom door:

1. "It scares me to have strangers stay here, especially when they're drunk. Can we talk about it?"
2. "Anything could happen when someone that neither one

of us knows very well is sleeping over. It makes me really uncomfortable, and I want to talk to you about it."

3. "It makes me nervous to wake up and find some stranger on the couch. Before that happens again, can we talk about it?"

4. "I trust you, but I don't trust some of the people you bring home. Can we work out some agreement about when and who stays over?"

5. "These rooms are so small that I can't help but be affected by who you bring back here. When you bring home a complete stranger, it makes me feel really unsafe."

Excuse Me, Do You Live Here?

"I came home one night to find my roommate's friends eating my food. My roommate apologized, but she never offered to pay me back. Another time, I found my computer on when I know I turned it off, and someone had obviously been sitting on my bed and using my pillow. I felt like her friends were into all my stuff and had no regard for privacy."

—ELLEN, AGE 20

Does it feel like your roommate's friends have moved in without consulting you? They've made themselves right at home. They eat your food, hog the TV, and sack out on your bed. Just like dealing with a girlfriend who visits too often, you have a right to ask your roommate to not have friends over all the time.

When you're dealing with a group, it can feel like you're outnumbered and getting ganged up on, so make sure to have the conversation when you and your roommate are alone. Keep the focus on your personal space, not whether or not you like the people. It's helpful to have examples of what you feel is crossing the line into your privacy and what you want to have happen. For example, if you mark your food in the fridge with stickers, what will happen if other people help themselves anyway? Do you want your food replaced, do you want to be reimbursed, or is an apology enough?

How to Break the Ice

If you feel your space is being invaded, here are some ideas on what you can say to your roommate:

1. "When your friends hang out here so much, I feel like I don't have any room to breathe. How about we designate some guest-free times?"

2. "I'd like to talk about what's okay and what's not when we have friends over. What's off-limits to you?"

3. "I noticed that your friends ate some of my food when they were over. I like your friends, but when they take things and don't replace them it hurts my wallet. How should we handle it if it happens again?"

4. "My things are really important to me, and it bugs me when other people sit on my bed or touch my stuff. How do you think we should handle friends in our room?"

5. "What do you think is a fair way to handle things if one of our friends breaks/uses something we consider personal?"

Although your roommate can't control a friend's behavior, rude habits, or lack of common courtesy, your roommate is ultimately responsible for his guests. If your roommate's friends are a problem, your roommate needs to deal with it—not you.

It Ain't My Fault

Your roommate may try and dodge responsibility by telling you, "I didn't do it; talk to so and so." While it's true we aren't responsible for other people's behavior, you and your roommate are accountable for the people you allow into the room and what happens while they are there. That includes letting visitors know what's okay and what's off limits. It's not your job to track down your roommate's friends to tell them how to behave or to get reimbursed for something. Hold your roommate accountable, and she can figure out how to replace it if something is stolen or broken.

But It's Our Problem

If you've made your feelings clear, and your roommate keeps inviting back certain individuals who cross the boundaries, by all means tell your RA. You should not have to tolerate people in your room who don't respect your rights. Here is how you can respond if your roommate tries to weasel out of the responsibility of talking to his friends:

1. "I know you didn't personally eat my food, but they're your friends, not mine. So I'd like you to talk about it with them."

2. "I don't feel it's fair that my stuff gets broken, and I'm the one who is responsible for making sure it gets fixed. I'd appreciate it if you'd talk to your friends."

3. "I don't know the people involved, but you do. Please talk to them so we can fix the problem."

4. "It's not my responsibility to tell your friends how to act, but if you want me to be there when you talk to them, I will."

5. "What I care about most is that my stuff gets replaced and that my things aren't touched in the future. How do you want to handle that?"

6. "Since I don't really know your friends, I think it's best that you talk to them and work something out."

Making it clear that you hold your roommate accountable for talking to her friends takes away any gray area. It's also possible that your roommate may decide it's not worth having those individuals over anymore!

Meet the Parents

"My roommate has overly protective parents. When he moved in, they wanted to know who their son was living with, so they came right out and asked me a bunch of personal questions. They wanted to know if I had a girlfriend, if we had sex, if I used drugs, and if I drank alcohol."

—MARK, AGE 21

A roommate's overly involved parents can make you feel like you're *marrying* the person instead of just agreeing to share a room! Of course you don't have to answer any questions you don't want to. It's best if you respectfully defer rather than be rude. A lot of people are very close to their parents, and some rely more heavily on parental advice than others. So, if you disrespect the parents, your roommate could hold a grudge. The other side is that your roommate could be completely humiliated by his parents' frankness and would appreciate being saved from even more embarrassment. It's okay to make a joke (at your expense), try to laugh it off, and then change the subject.

How to Fend Off the Questions

Parental pressure can be intense—even when it's not coming from your own! If your roommate's parents are giving you the third degree, here are some ways you can politely decline to answer:

1. "I understand you want to know who your daughter is rooming with, and I'm sure we won't have any problems getting along."
2. "Wow! You caught me off guard; I didn't study for this quiz—I better hit the books!"
3. "I'm not comfortable talking about that subject, but I'd be glad to tell you a little about my family and my major."
4. "I hope this is multiple choice. It's too early in the morning for me to think!"
5. "Oh wait, I was going to ask you questions first. How was your trip? Have you ever seen the campus before?"
6. "Did my parents send you here undercover? I'll have to talk to them about that! Anyway, it's nice to meet you."

Deflect probing questions with as much humor and politeness as you can manage. If they persist, tactfully excuse yourself and say you need to study or run to a class.

Spying on Junior

Some parents like to call and "check in." Those calls can quickly turn into a barrage of questions about their child: Do you know where he is? Has she been studying? What's going on with his girlfriend? She's not drinking too much, is she? Aside from not answering the phone anymore, what do you do? It's best not to get in the middle of any relationship, whether it's reporting to the parents or covering for your roommate by lying. Unless there's a serious health concern that might make you consider contacting your roommate's parents (see Chapter 11), let your roommate handle his own affairs.

Exit Strategy

The last thing you want to do is get in the middle of any issues between your roommate and her parents. You risk breaking your roommate's trust, and at the end of the day, it's your roommate you have to live with. Here is how you can exit a conversation with your roommate's parents before you get in too deep:

1. "I'm not the best person to talk to about that, but I'd be glad to leave a message."
2. "I don't know where he is, but I'll leave a note that you called."
3. "I'm sure your daughter can answer these questions better than I could. The best time to reach her is before 10 A.M."
4. "Sounds like you really need to talk to your son about that, so I'll make sure to let him know you called."
5. "I don't have the answers to all your questions, but I'll leave a message that you called."

6. "I don't really know her schedule that well, but I think she usually carries a cell phone. Why don't you try her there?"

Use your best judgment when dealing with your roommate's parents. Extend the same courtesies that you would want for your parents and yourself.

Tips to Remember

- If your roommate's dates see more of your room than you do, speak up! Talk to your roommate about having consideration for your rights too.

- It's not your responsibility to come up with other locations for your roommate to hook up, so just smile and shrug when she says, "Where else are we supposed to go?"

- You and your roommate are responsible for the people you bring into the room and are ultimately accountable for what happens when they are there.

- Some parents can become a little too up close and personal when it comes to getting to know their child's roommate. If you get the third degree, you don't have to answer anything. But it's better to politely defer rather than respond rudely.

To learn more about setting boundaries, visit your campus counseling center or read *Where to Draw the Line: How to Set Healthy Boundaries Every Day* by Anne Katherine (Fireside, 2000).

11

I Think My Roommate
Has a Serious Problem

Quick Quiz: True or False

Your roommate sleeps all the time and doesn't want to leave the room.	T/F
Your roommate talks about "ending it all."	T/F
Your roommate is losing a lot of weight and is obsessed with exercise.	T/F

Score:

1 T: You're waiting for your roommate to stop acting so weird.

2 Ts: Your roommate's behaviors are getting worse, and it has you totally stressed.

3 Ts: You're not sure who needs professional help more: you or your roommate.

She's Not Crazy, Just a Little Unwell

"My roommate's mood swings are horrible. One minute she's cool, the next she's ready to bite my head off. Sometimes she's in a bad mood for weeks. She cries for no reason. When I ask her what's wrong, she says she doesn't know."

—MEGAN, AGE 22

Crazy. Freak. Wacko. Nuts. Psycho. There are lots of disrespectful ways to describe someone who's not mentally well. It's hard for anyone to admit she needs help, knowing she might get instantly labeled. But mental illness can happen to anyone. Academic stress, traumatic events like a bad breakup, or feelings of anxiety are a few examples of experiences that can be difficult for some to handle. Mental problems are scary because they are unseen. No one thinks twice about visiting a doctor for a few stitches. When pain is mental or emotional, people tend to get secretive, feel ashamed, and assume they should be able to just deal with it. The majority of people suffering from mental illnesses are regular people who've hit a rough spot and who need help learning how to cope.

Mental health is a lot like physical health. There are certain things everyone can do to stay in shape, and not everyone maintains the same level of fitness. Some people eat right and exercise, others exist on a diet of pizza, nachos, chicken wings, and beer. Bodies are different too. Some people have allergies, asthma, or poor eyesight; others have no problems at all. When flu season hits, some students never get sick, while others spend the entire semester in the health center.

The same differences exist in mental health. People aren't all built the same. Some respond to stress better than others. When something hurts, everyone has a unique way of dealing with it. It all depends on how a person takes care of herself. The most important thing to know about mental illness is that it is treatable.

No Playing Doctor

As you read symptoms of the most common mental health problems, remember that only a professional can diagnose someone. As a roommate or a friend, all you can do is offer support. Ultimately, your roommate is responsible for his own behavior and treatment. That doesn't mean that living with someone who is struggling is not incredibly stressful! Your roommate's actions can have a huge impact on you. Sharing your concerns and how the situation is affecting you is a good approach. But, be careful of being judgmental. A person suffering from depression is not lazy, and someone with an eating disorder doesn't need you to be a food intake monitor. Saying, "You just need to snap out of it," does more damage than good.

Avoid labeling. Your roommate may already feel guilty or ashamed. Hearing that you think her behavior is not normal only makes things worse. You wouldn't judge your roommate if she had a physical disability. Oftentimes, a mental problem can be just as debilitating. Be open-minded and seek out more information.

Common Mental Health Issues on Campus

When it comes to mental health, college students can struggle just as much as any other population. Some of the most common mental health issues found on college campuses include depression, suicide, anxiety, eating disorders, substance abuse, and self-injury. Remember, if you're worried that you or your roommate may be experiencing any of the symptoms listed in this section, do not try and diagnose it yourself! Seek help from a qualified professional immediately.

Depression: More Than the Blahs

"I was always a straight-A student, but I started to feel overwhelmed. It was like I was drowning and forgot how to swim. I kept it to myself for a long time, because I was embarrassed. Finally, my roommate suggested I see a counselor, and that's when I found out I had depression."

—AMELIA, AGE 19

Everyone feels down or blue once in awhile. Especially during difficult times, it's normal to feel sad or discouraged. But when those feelings persist for two weeks or longer, it could be depression. It's a common illness that affects an estimated 19 million Americans—that's nearly one in ten! It's also one of the most under-diagnosed illnesses on college campuses. The symptoms can come on so slowly that one day, a person realizes that he can't remember the last time he felt good. Here are some warning signs for depression:

- Persistent sad, anxious, or empty mood
- Feelings of hopelessness, pessimism
- Feelings of guilt, worthlessness, helplessness
- Loss of interest or enjoyment in things that used to be fun
- Decreased energy, fatigue
- Restlessness, irritability
- Difficulty concentrating, remembering, or making decisions
- Trouble sleeping, or oversleeping
- Appetite or weight changes
- Thoughts of suicide

Many students suffer needlessly. Depression is often very treatable. Not everyone experiences every symptom, and the severity can vary over time. Through counseling and, in some cases, medication, the majority of people notice significant improvement.

How to Help Someone Suffering from Depression

If your roommate is suffering from depression, encourage her to seek professional help. Depression can feel like a black tunnel that has no end in sight. The most important thing you can do is to provide hope. Let the person know it is treatable.

Also, offer emotional support, patience, and understanding. Depression can be as painful as any physical illness. Telling a depressed person to "snap out of it" is like telling someone with two broken legs to get up and walk. Be supportive and engage him in conversation and activities even if your efforts are met with protest or resistance. The most important thing you can do for someone with depression is to make sure the person isn't isolated.

Suicide: Depression at Its Worst

"When my roommate's girlfriend broke up with him, he took it really hard. He kept talking about how he didn't want to live without her."

—EMILIO, AGE 20

Thoughts of suicide are usually a sign of severe depression. It's scary to be around someone who talks about killing himself. Most of us don't ever want to think about it. But you can't ignore suicidal threats.

How to Help Someone Threatening Suicide

Many people threatening suicide make their intentions known ahead of time. Pay attention, and really listen to your roommate. If there are any hints or indications that your roommate intends to commit suicide, here's what to keep in mind:

- Take threats seriously!
- Stay with the person and talk. Do not leave her alone. Talking

about suicide will *not* make it worse—you won't be planting ideas that weren't there already. And you won't be encouraging dying. Giving the person a chance to talk honestly may save her life.

- Ask if he has a suicide plan. This is a tough conversation, but crucial. The more detailed the plan, the more likely something will happen.
- Ask if she has swallowed pills; if so, call 911 immediately.
- Report your roommate's behavior to your RA and a campus counselor. This is not the time to keep secrets.

Talk of suicide is a cry for help that needs to be addressed *immediately*. It's an indication that the person is experiencing deep despair and immense pain. It takes someone to intervene to help a suicidal individual find a way out of the darkness and restore hope for the future.

Anxiety: More Than a Case of the Nerves

"My roommate could never relax. She was always on edge and worried constantly. I tried to calm her down and reassure her, but nothing I said made a difference. It made me tense to be around her."

—NICOLE, AGE 20

We've all felt anxious—the nerves you get before a big test, or before a first date. Maybe the thought of having to speak in front of a small group gives you butterflies in your stomach, makes your heart beat faster, and your palms sweaty. A certain level of anxiety is healthy. It's what gives people motivation to do well, and it can help provide protection from danger. But an anxiety disorder causes the opposite effects. The feelings of worry and nervousness are so overwhelming that they can keep a person from coping and disrupt daily life.

Symptoms of Panic Disorders

There are several types of anxiety disorders including panic attacks, phobias, obsessive-compulsive disorder, and generalized anxiety. All are treatable with the help of counseling and, in some cases, medication. Here are the warning signs for two such disorders, which are the most common.

Panic attacks (at least four of the following symptoms are experienced)
- Racing or pounding heartbeat
- Chest pains
- Dizziness
- Nausea
- Difficulty breathing
- Feeling flushed, chills, or sweating
- Tingling or numbness in the hands
- Dreamlike sensations
- Fear of losing control and doing something embarrassing
- Fear of dying
- Sense of impending doom

Symptoms for Generalized Anxiety Disorder
- At least six months of persistent and excessive anxiety about a number of events and activities
- Restlessness, feeling keyed up, or on edge

- Easily fatigued
- Difficulty concentrating or mind going blank
- Irritability
- Muscle tension
- Sleep disturbances—either sleeping too much, or not enough

Don't jump to conclusions if your roommate occasionally experiences these symptoms. College is a stressful time. Everyone has a bout of irritability, sadness, or sleeplessness from time to time. But experiencing several of these symptoms on a regular basis indicates a need for help.

How to Help Someone Suffering from an Anxiety Disorder

Encourage your roommate to seek professional help. Anxiety is treatable through counseling and, in some cases, medication. If you are around someone experiencing a panic attack, remind the person to breathe deeply. People have a tendency during a panic attack to take shallow breaths and hyperventilate, which makes the attack last longer. Breathing deeply from the belly will help the person calm down.

You can also help a person suffering from panic disorders by encouraging her to exercise and/or by being her workout buddy.

Moving the body aerobically is a great way to manage stress, and studies have shown that exercise boosts chemicals in the brain that promote feelings of calmness and well-being.

While you should encourage someone who is suffering from depression or anxiety to get out, have fun, and socialize, *do not* encourage use of drugs or alcohol. People who are experiencing anxiety or depression often use drugs or alcohol to self-medicate, which can be a dangerous situation. Also, alcohol is a depressant and can cause a drop in blood sugar. The body then responds by producing more adrenaline, which fuels anxiety.

Eating Disorders: A Struggle for Control

"My roommate was obsessed with her weight. At one point she existed on two Tic Tacs for breakfast, two crackers for lunch, and an apple for dinner. She only weighed about 80 pounds, but she was still convinced she was fat."

—LACI, AGE 18

Weight fluctuations are common in college. Gaining the average fifteen pounds, or the "Freshman 15," is easy to do between cafeteria food, all-night study sessions, too much beer, and not enough exercise. But when food and weight becomes an obsession, it can turn deadly. Eating disorders affect both men and women. They include anorexia nervosa (self-starvation) and bulimia (binging and purging).

Eating disorders are not about food. They are expressions of perceived social pressure, poor body image, feeling a lack of control, extreme stress, and emotional needs. The illness can be devastating and warps the way a person sees herself. Those with eating disorders often experience enormous feelings of guilt and shame. Some may exercise compulsively, avoid social situations involving food, lie about how much food has been consumed, or only eat in private.

Eating disorders are treatable, and the sooner a person gets help the better. Anorexia nervosa can lead to death from cardiac arrest and electrolyte imbalance. Here are the warning signs:

Symptoms of Anorexia Nervosa
- Resistance to maintaining a weight that's considered normal for age and height
- Intense fear of gaining weight or becoming fat, even though underweight
- Distorted body image
- For women, absent or irregular menstrual cycles

Symptoms of Bulimia
- Binge eating (eating a large amount of food within a two-hour period)
- Feeling a lack of control while binging—like you can't stop yourself
- Purging by self-induced vomiting, laxatives, or diet pills
- Broken blood vessels in the eyes, tooth decay (from vomiting)
- Exercising excessively

Try and be sensitive to the fact that exposure to certain media can cause increased anxiety for someone with an eating disorder. TV shows promoting plastic surgery and magazines featuring airbrushed pictures of models present images of perfection that are impossible to attain.

How to Help Someone Suffering from an Eating Disorder

If you suspect your roommate has an eating disorder, encourage her to seek professional help. Discuss your concerns in a sensitive, supportive way. Keep your comments focused on her health and how it's affecting your relationship rather than on weight or appearance. Avoid assuming the role of "food police." This will only make her more secretive. If you feel her weight is dangerously low, report your concerns to the campus counseling center.

People suffering from eating disorders can be in denial. Be prepared for your friend rejecting you or your observations when you first try to address them with her. Stay open for future conversations, and get outside help if you think things have gotten to a crisis point.

Substance Abuse: Party 'till You Drop (Out)

"My roommate parties all the time. For awhile it was fun, but he doesn't know when to stop. He gets stoned every day and skips class, and his personality has changed. When I mentioned it, he exploded and told me to mind my own business."

—SEAN, AGE 22

For some, the exposure to drugs and alcohol during college can feel like overwhelming pressure to experiment. It can be hard to know when a person has crossed the line between having a good time and having a problem. In a college atmosphere, where some feel getting trashed every weekend is considered normal, how do you know how much is too much? Living with someone who goes on regular binges is very stressful. He can be loud, obnoxious, and up at all hours, and cleanup the next day isn't pretty!

Alcohol and chemical dependency can sneak up on a person, developing over a semester or two. Besides the legal ramifications of underage drinking and using controlled substances, one of the first indicators of trouble is ignoring academic work. Skipping classes and not studying soon results in poor grades. There may be other irresponsible behaviors, like not showing up for work, not paying bills on time, or sabotaging relationships. Here are more of the warning signs:

- Needing more and more of the substance to achieve the same desired effect
- Experiencing withdrawal effects when not taking the substance, such as uncontrollable shaking, sweating, nausea, or delirium
- Investing a lot of time and energy in getting the substance, using it, or recovering from it
- Giving up or decreasing important activities for substance use
- Using the substance despite awareness of how doing so is negatively impacting grades, finances, and/or relationships

Most people want to believe they can stop at any time. They say things like, "I just do it on weekends," or "Once I graduate, I'll quit." But for those who've become dependent, it's not so easy. They need professional help.

How to Help Someone Suffering from Substance Dependence

Substance abuse is a problem. Don't blow it off by rationalizing that it's college and everybody drinks or that your roommate comes from a good family, is only eighteen years old, goes to a great school, etc., and therefore can't have a drug problem. Don't cover for the person or make excuses. For example, if she skips work, and the boss calls, hand the phone over rather than make up a story.

Choose the right time to talk about the problem. Wait until your roommate is sober, and both of you are calm. Let her know how her choices have affected you, giving specific examples such as, "It really scared me when you drank so much last weekend that I couldn't wake you up."

Although your first concern may be for your roommate's well-being, your roommate's substance abuse problem affects you too. Decide where your boundaries are. Let him know exactly what you plan to do to protect yourself—whether that means not getting in the car together when he has been drinking or reporting use of illegal drugs in your dorm room. Above all, encourage your roommate to seek professional help. Substance dependence is treatable.

Self-Injury: Finding a Way to Cope

"I noticed a bunch of scars on my roommate's wrists. When I asked her where they came from, she said she did it. She said cutting made her feel better. I'm scared she's going to kill herself."

—JEN, AGE 20

It's hard to understand why someone would hurt herself, but for some it's a way to cope with traumatic events or severe emotional pain. The person is not "crazy," but rather just never learned appropriate ways to express intense feelings. Some of the most common ways to self-injure include cutting, burning, hitting, scratching, and pulling hair. A person who self-injures usually does so in private. She does not typically flaunt or brag about injuries. You may not even be aware of your roommate's behavior unless you notice scars or wounds.

Although some men self-injure, the behavior is more prevalent amongst women. The reasons vary. Some who self-mutilate say it helps to release pain, while others say it offers distraction from traumatic memories. For some, self-injury gives a sense of control. Others are numb to emotion, and self-injury gives them a way to feel something.

Symptoms of Self-Injury

The biggest misconception is that self-injury is an attempt to commit suicide. The person in question may feel so bad that he has had suicidal thoughts, but generally the two are unrelated. In most cases, the act of self-injury is an attempt to cope with those intense feelings, not die. Here are the warning signs of self-injury:

- Compulsive need to injure oneself by cutting, burning, hitting, scratching, or pulling hair
- Re-injuring old wounds so they don't heal
- Scarring, usually on arms, wrists, legs, abdomen, head, or chest
- Attempts to hide arms or other body parts where injury occurred
- Hoarding of sharp objects like razors
- Person experiences a high from doing it
- Consuming thoughts of self-injury, or the behavior interrupts normal daily functioning
- In most cases, there is no intention of killing oneself, only to cope with or release intense feelings of pain
- Usually self-injures when alone

The reasons for self-injury are varied and complex. It can be scary and uncomfortable to be around someone who hurts herself in this way. Even though it may seem to you that your roommate is causing herself increased pain, self-injurers are attempting to diminish their pain. That doesn't mean that you shouldn't take the problem very seriously.

How to Help Someone Suffering from Self-Injury

As difficult as it may be, do not attempt to stop or control your roommate's self-injury. You are not responsible for her behavior, and by interfering with her way of coping, you could do more harm than good. Trying to hide or take away self-injury tools, giving ultimatums, or "guilt tripping" your roommate into stopping only encourages more self-hatred and more self-injury. Instead, support your roommate by helping her express feelings and offering to listen without judgment. Keep your support consistent—in other words, don't offer the most attention only after an episode. Purchase a journal for your roommate to use as a safe way to express feelings. Encourage her to seek professional help. Self-injury is treatable. It can be extremely frightening and disturbing to be around this type of behavior, and it's important that you acknowledge the emotions it evokes in you. Do not hesitate to talk to your RA or see a counselor to process your feelings and request additional guidance on how best to support your roommate.

How to Approach Your Roommate and the Problem

If you suspect your roommate suffers from one of the illnesses discussed in this chapter, educate yourself as much as you can. Here are some ways to approach a person who may be in trouble:

1. "When I don't see you get out of bed or eat, it's scary. It seems like you've felt this way for awhile. Maybe it's time to get help."

2. "I noticed a bunch of laxatives in the bathroom. It scares me when I hear you vomiting. I'm worried about your losing so much weight."

3. "When you talk about killing yourself, it freaks me out. I don't know if you're kidding or not, but I don't think it's a joke. I think it's time to talk to a professional."

4. "I noticed that you're having more and more panic attacks. It seems like your stress level is getting worse. There are people on campus you can talk to so that you don't have to feel this way anymore."

5. "I care about you. Have you stopped taking your medication? I can really see a change in your mood."

6. "Your drinking is affecting me. I can't handle any more calls at 3 A.M. or finding you passed out in the hallway. It's stressing me out. It seems like your drinking has become a problem. Maybe it's time to talk to someone."

If your roommate is having serious problems, visit your campus counseling center and discuss your concerns. Sessions are confidential, and you don't have to name names. The counselor can help you better understand the illness and offer appropriate ways to support your roommate.

My Roommate Won't Listen

Your roommate may deny there's a problem or get angry that you said anything. On the other hand, your roommate may have a sense of relief that things are out in the open. Ignoring the problem won't make it go away. If you really feel your roommate is in trouble, it's worth the risk of having him get mad at you. Again, your roommate's choices are not your responsibility. But it may ease your mind to know that you did what you could.

If she won't listen and appears to be getting worse, notify a qualified person on campus. Share your concerns with a counselor, doctor, nurse, professor, hall director, or RA. Being the only one who knows is a big burden to carry. By talking with someone else, you can get another opinion. This may be the first time you've had to deal with someone who needs help, but campus staff has seen it before. They'll have a better idea of what to do.

Should you tell your roommate's parents? That's a decision only you can make. You may feel strongly that the parents need to know what's going on, and it's the quickest way to get action. From the parents' point of view, they probably would be very thankful for the call and would want to know immediately if their daughter is in trouble. If you were the parent, wouldn't you want to know?

The risk is that you'll get stuck in the middle. That's an added responsibility and could put you in an uncomfortable position. If you know your roommate doesn't have a good relationship with his parents, it may feel like a betrayal to give private information. If you're not sure what to do, a safe route is to contact a campus professional and let that person make the tough decisions.

I'm Only Trying to Help You

It's hard for people to hear that they have a problem, particularly if it involves substance abuse, an eating disorder, depression, or anxiety. Even the most caring intervention can be interpreted in a negative way. Here's how you can respond if your roommate is in denial or gets mad:

1. "I'm bringing this up because I care about you. I want you to know that I'm here if you want to talk."
2. "I care enough about you to risk your getting mad at me. I'm concerned for your safety."
3. "I was scared you'd get mad, but it scares me more to see the shape you're in."
4. "I know you don't want to talk about it now, but I picked up some information. I'll leave it here if you want to look at it."
5. "I consider myself a friend, and that's why I said something. It hurts me to see you not doing well."
6. "I know you don't think anything's wrong. But, I think it's fair to share what I've noticed and how it's affecting me."

Living in such close quarters, you may notice that your roommate is struggling before other people suspect anything. By choosing to say something early, you can encourage your roommate to address problems before they snowball.

Counseling Myths and Facts

"I tried to get my roommate to go to counseling, but he's convinced it's only for people who are really messed up. Plus he can't understand how talking about your problems can make a difference. He said it would make him feel worse."

—MARK, AGE 18

What goes on in counseling anyway? How can it help? Does it matter which counselor someone sees? Most people have no idea—and that's what scares them. You should have some information handy if you plan on advising your roommate or friend to seek help.

Campus counseling staffs typically have at least one psychologist, several licensed counselors, and some grad students completing required internships. Students can request to meet with a certain counselor that they feel would be a good match. If it turns out a student is not comfortable with a counselor, he can ask to see someone else—nobody's feelings will get hurt! Counselors understand that they don't click with everyone. Following are some other common concerns and misunderstandings about counseling.

Myth #1: I'll have to lie on a couch and talk about my dreams.

Every counselor has his or her own style, but there isn't any long-term psychoanalysis going on in a campus counseling center. In general, students can expect to fill out an intake form regarding personal history and current problems. During the first session, the counselor will get to know a student, ask what brought her in, and talk about what she'd like to change to feel better.

Myth #2: My problems aren't big enough to need counseling.

People don't have to be sick to want to feel better. If a student is frustrated enough that his problem is having a negative effect on his life, that is reason enough for counseling. Sometimes people just need to vent. Just like physical sickness, it's better to address things sooner rather than later.

Myth #3: If I go to a counselor, everyone will find out.

Except for a few specific situations, what students share with counselors is private and confidential. Parents, professors, or other students do not have access to other students' mental health records. However, if a counselor feels that a student might cause harm to himself or someone else, confidentiality can be broken. Counselors usually discuss this in the first session.

Myth #4: Counselors give advice and tell you exactly what to do.

Friends give advice; counselors help people find their own solutions. That means that counselors will not tell students what to do. Instead, a counselor asks a student questions to help him discover what he can do for himself.

Myth #5: Talking to a stranger can't change anything.

A counselor offers an objective viewpoint without judgment. Professionals offer expert insight that friends and family can't. Sometimes it's easier talking to someone who accepts a person for who she is, without a lot of history getting in the way.

Myth #6: Talking about my problems will only make them worse.

In order to solve something, it must be acknowledged. But counselors don't dwell on problems. They focus on solutions. They'll help you figure out what's causing a situation and suggest better ways to deal with it.

Myth #7: If I go once, they'll make me keep coming back.

Counseling is completely voluntary. Students can quit at any time. A counselor's goal is to help a student feel better, not to keep him in counseling for life.

Myth #8: The counselor will tell me I'm mentally ill and put me on medication.

Counselors are qualified to diagnose and treat mental illnesses, but not prescribe medication. In some situations, a counselor may refer a student to a psychiatrist to discuss drug treatment in addition to talk therapy. Whether or not the student takes medication is always her choice.

Myth #9: If I admit I need counseling, I'll be branded for life.

Asking for help when struggling is the smart thing to do, not a sign of personal weakness. Mental illness is treatable. Counseling helps people address their issues now so that they're *not* branded for life.

Myth #10: I can't afford it.

Most colleges provide students a limited number of sessions for free or a small charge. They can also provide referrals to practitioners that charge reduced fees.

Admitting a need for help can be scary, especially if a person's friends and family have a negative view of counseling. However, not all problems are meant to be handled solo. Most people would rather live with the short-term discomfort of seeking counseling than the long-term pain of dealing with a burden they can't manage, particularly those which jeopardize relationships and health.

Just because you're trying to get help for your roommate doesn't mean you should overlook your own needs. If you're stressed or frustrated to the point that it's having a negative impact on your life, you may want to consider counseling for yourself. When your roommate won't change destructive behavior, it can invade your life so much that you feel as if you have no control or all your issues are on the back burner. Counseling is something you can do for yourself that puts you back in charge of your life.

Tips to Remember

- Mental illness can happen to anyone. The majority of people suffering from mental illness are regular people who've hit a rough spot in life and need help coping.
- Mental illness is treatable! There's no need to suffer in silence. Asking for help is not a sign of personal weakness.
- As a roommate, you can only offer support. It's not your job to judge or assume responsibility for someone else's behavior.

- Help is available through your campus counseling center. Sessions are free or low cost and in most cases, confidential.
- Living with a roommate who is not mentally well is stressful! Seek out counseling if you need support or help coping.

If your roommate is dealing with a mental health issue, encourage him to schedule an appointment with a counselor on campus. In addition, the following resources can provide more information:

- To learn more about depression, take the National Mental Health Association's online depression screening at *www. depression-screening.org.*
- To learn more about suicide, visit the Jed Foundation Web site at *www.jedfoundation.org.* For help with someone who is threatening to commit suicide, call 911 or the National Hopeline Network Suicide Hotline at 1-800-SUICIDE (1-800-784-2433).
- To learn more about anxiety, contact the Anxiety Disorders Association of America at *www.adaa.org.*
- For additional help with eating disorders, contact the National Eating Disorders Association at *www.edap.org.*
- The National Drug and Alcohol Treatment Referral Routing Service at 800-662-HELP can provide more information on substance abuse.
- And to find out more about self-injury visit the American Self-Harm Information Clearinghouse at *www.selfinjury.org.* You can also call the SAFE Alternatives Program at 1-800-DON'T-CUT (800-366-8288).

12

Asking for Help: When to Involve Others

Quick Quiz: True or False

Your roommate doesn't understand where you're coming
from, no matter how many times you explain yourself.   T/F

Even though you try to talk calmly to your roommate,
 the conversation always escalates into a fight.   T/F

Your roommate's behavior is scaring you.   T/F

Score:

1 T: You've started talking to the wall since it's the same as talking to your roommate, minus the attitude.

2 Ts: Friends have stopped asking how things are going because the stories about your "impossible roommate" are getting old.

3 Ts: You're sleeping with the lights on because you don't trust your roommate for a second (plus it has the added bonus of getting on his nerves).

I'm Telling!

"I've done everything I can, but my roommate and I can't get past our problems. I know I should tell my RA, but I'm afraid of being a nark."

—GERI, AGE 18

If talking to your roommate is like talking to a brick wall, it may be
time to get someone else involved. The question is who, how, and
when? Residence life staffs encourage you to go to your RA for help,

but not before trying to work things out on your own first. Your RA can mediate or give you ideas on what to say and help you practice confrontations, but you and your roommate are ultimately responsible for solving your own problems. The mistake most students make is either waiting too long to ask for help or going to the RA immediately without talking to their roommates first. If you wait too long, the problem escalates to the point where neither side is willing to budge, while going behind your roommate's back can hurt a relationship beyond repair.

Knowing when to bring in a third party is a judgment call, but if your roommate situation involves illegal activities, jeopardizing your personal safety, or anything against university policy, talk to your RA immediately.

Before You Go to the RA

Resident advisors are there to help you. Often, they have special training (and personal perspective) in helping students cope with personal, academic, and roommate conflicts. However, if you involve your RA, do it after you've exhausted other options. Here are the steps you should try before involving your RA:

- Discuss your concerns with your roommate.
- Emphasize your desire to work things out.
- Give several concrete examples of what is bothering you.
- Share how the situation has impacted you.
- Allow your roommate to respond and share his concerns.
- Talk about a solution and put it down in writing.

If you've done all these things and you've still got problems, then it's time to go to your RA. Be prepared to share the steps you've already taken and why your attempts at resolution didn't work. Give examples of how your roommate's behavior is bothering you, and stay away from making assumptions about his motivations. For example, you might say, "I can't study when he cranks up the volume on his stereo," but leave out, "he does it because he's selfish and doesn't care about anyone but himself." Your RA might also ask what else is going on in your life, because sometimes roommate problems are often symptoms of larger issues.

Top Ten Ways to Get on Your RA's Bad Side

Keep in mind that your RA is human! You should expect her to listen without judgment, remain neutral, and refer you to another person such as a counselor or academic advisor if the situation is beyond her skills. But you can make that really hard to do if you're not being cooperative or reasonable. If you're demanding or refusing to go through the normal channels (including talking to your roommate), you'll end up with two enemies instead of one. These are the top ten ways to get on your RA's bad side:

1. Get as many people involved in your situation as possible by gossiping to friends and floormates and encouraging them to take sides.
2. Have your parents become overly involved by calling the RA, Hall Director, and Area Coordinator and insisting that something be done immediately.
3. Decide that you're moving out and start making plans before you even talk to your RA.

4. Absolutely refuse to compromise.

5. Avoid talking in person by only communicating through IM and e-mail.

6. Say, "Nothing," or "Everything's fine," when your RA asks what the problem is, then complain behind his back.

7. Don't even talk to your RA, go right to the Area Coordinator, or worse yet the College President.

8. Accuse your RA of favoring your roommate and masterminding the conspiracy against you.

9. Expect your RA to fix the problem and assume you won't have to do a thing.

10. Tell your RA that your roommate, "looks at me funny," and expect him to know exactly what you mean.

Although your RA should be available to help you, keep in mind that he is also responsible for helping ten to forty other floormates, attending class, studying, working part-time, or managing extracurricular activities, not to mention handling personal issues. Do as much of the heavy lifting yourself before approaching your RA to mediate the situation.

We Need Help

The decision to tell your RA about your situation should not be used as a threat against your roommate. Instead, if you can't reach an agreement, openly discuss it as an option and invite your roommate to go with you. The more you involve your roommate in the process the less likely it is that you'll be labeled a whiner.

How to Break the Ice

You shouldn't share information with your RA that has not already been discussed with your roommate! Passive-aggressive behavior will only make the situation worse and kill your credibility. Here's how you can suggest to your roommate that your RA needs to get involved:

1. "I'm all out of ideas on how to solve this. Unless you have something else, I think it's time for us to talk to our RA."

2. "This argument isn't going anywhere, so let's ask our RA for help. There isn't anything I plan to say that I haven't already discussed with you."

3. "This isn't working with just the two of us. Will you go with me to talk to our RA?"

4. "We're having the same argument over and over. Why don't we get an outside opinion?"

5. "I've tried everything and I don't know what else to do. I'm going to talk to our RA. Would you come too?"

Going to your RA can be a positive move as long as you involve your roommate from the beginning. It shows good will on your part to treat your roommate as an equal partner in solving issues rather than as an enemy.

What If My Roommate Goes Behind My Back?

It's never fun to hear from someone else that your roommate thinks you're a problem, especially when your roommate forgot to mention it to you. Talk about feeling burned! It makes you wonder what else is being said behind your back. The best way to handle the situation is to stay open and honest. Ask to meet with your RA and roommate together so everyone's hearing the same story.

In the Dark?

If your roommate is telling others you're a problem, you have a right to know about it. However, don't fly off the handle if you find out that your roommate has gone to a third party without you. Instead, express your willingness to work things out and ask that she talk to you first in the future. Here's how you can respond if your roommate leaves you out of the loop:

1. "I want to work things out, so will you come to me first in the future?"

2. "I heard from another student that you have issues with me. I'm willing to talk about them, but is there a reason I wasn't told first?"

3. "When you go to other people about our problems it really upsets me. Can we agree to tell each other first if there is an issue?"

4. "I would appreciate knowing in advance that we are going to involve the RA, otherwise it feels like I'm being ganged up on. I want to work with everyone to solve this."

5. "It's important to me that we're honest with each other. Next time, will you please give me a chance to handle things first before going to someone else?"

Since neither you nor your roommate can change what's already happened, it does no good to keep rehashing the past. Focus on how things can be handled better in the future.

Buddy System

"I didn't bother talking to my RA because she's best friends with my room-mate. There's no way my RA would listen to my side of the story without being biased. Plus, I feel like anything I told my RA would get right back to my roommate."

—LESLIE, AGE 18

It's your RA's job to be there for everyone on her floor and remain a neutral party in disputes. However, despite your RA's job description and training, it's still possible to feel like she is favoring your roommate because they are friends. Before you make any assumptions though, give your RA the benefit of the doubt. After all, that's how you're asking to be treated, right? If you approach the situation with your mind already made up that you're going to be treated unfairly, you'll be unlikely to accomplish anything.

Residence life staffs have a clear chain of command. It's important for you to respect the process, which can take time (that's why you need to address your issue right away). If you skip your RA and jump to the hall director, you'll probably be sent right back to talk with your RA. And how do you think that person will feel knowing that you went over her head? The same rules of open communication apply to dealing with your RA as they do with your roommate. Don't share new information with higher-ups that has not been discussed with your RA, and notify your RA that you're not satisfied and plan to take your concerns up the ladder. As always, stick to the facts. This means that unless you have hard evidence and specific examples of favoritism, don't even go there.

How to Break the Ice

Make sure you walk away with a plan of action and a timeline when you and your roommate meet with your RA. If things don't work out, follow up with your RA and give him the chance to intervene again. Then if nothing happens you can let him know you plan to take your concerns to the supervisor. Here's what you can say to your RA if you feel he is not taking appropriate action:

1. "I've done everything you suggested, but the situation still hasn't improved. I feel like it's time to ask someone else for help."

2. "I feel like my concerns are not being addressed. Is there anything else we can do or should I ask the hall director?"

3. "I was expecting some follow-up on my situation, but nothing has happened. Is there anything else you can suggest, or should I go to the hall director?"

4. "When I explain my side of the story, I don't feel like it's taken seriously. I really need help. Should I go to the hall director?"

5. "This is a big deal to me, and I don't feel like we're any closer to a solution. Can we ask another person to help?"

Bear in mind that no matter how diplomatic you are, your RA could take offense—and make life harder for you directly or indirectly by dealing with you as little as possible in the future. Be careful before burning any bridges. Having a roommate and an RA that you don't get along with could make your living situation even more challenging than it already is.

What If My Parents Want to Get Involved?

When things are not going well at school, it's natural to turn to your parents for support. Of course, sometimes they offer their opinion when you don't want it! While it's important to keep your parents up-to-date, be careful about enlisting them to fight your battles. It's expected that you're going to run into conflicts with your roommate as a normal part of the college experience. It's also expected that you learn how to get along with others and manage disagreements in the real world. So if your parents step in and take over an issue that you should be dealing with, you're losing out on practicing critical life skills—and not winning any friends with your roommate, RA, or college administration. Unless you've gone through the entire system and have been blatantly ignored, ask your parents to let you handle it.

Back Off Mom and Dad!

Here's what you can say if your parents are too eager to get involved:

1. "If things get too out of hand, I promise I'll let you know. For right now, please let me deal with it."
2. "I know you care about me, but I haven't tried everything yet. Please let me handle it for now."

3. "This is my responsibility. I need to learn how to solve my own problems."
4. "Thanks for your support, but if you get involved now it will make me feel like you don't trust me to handle this."
5. "Please don't call anybody yet. I need to learn how to do this on my own."

Sharing with your parents how you solved the situation is a good opportunity for them to see that you are capable of handling your own affairs, and it should help build their confidence in you for the future.

Tips to Remember

- Try to solve your own problems first. Discuss your concerns with your roommate, and only go to your RA if that does not improve the situation.

- Invite your roommate to go with you to talk to your RA instead of using it as a threat. Never share information with your RA that your roommate has not already heard from you first.

- Your RA can't solve all your problems and may not have the skills for every situation. Your RA has been trained to listen without judgment and respond to your concerns. But if you are uncooperative or unrealistic, it makes the job impossible.

- If your roommate and RA are friends, you still need to go through the system. Jumping the chain of command will only earn you enemies. If you still feel appropriate action has not been taken, then take it to the RA's supervisor.

- Colleges and universities expect you to get along with others and work out disagreements. Ask your parents for moral support, but don't ask them to fight your battles for you.

Review your school's Residence Life guidelines and expectations on the campus Web site. If you're an RA, find support and learn more about managing roommate conflicts from two great Web sites: *www.ResidentAssistant.com* and *www.ResLifePro.com.*

13

When to Call It Quits

Quick Quiz: True or False

You'd rather drop out of school than continue to
live with your roommate.   T/F

The situation with your roommate has taken over
your life.   T/F

You've made every possible effort to resolve your
situation and nothing has worked.   T/F

Score:

1 T: You know exactly how many days are left in the
semester—down to the minute.

2 Ts: You've already asked at least three other people if you
could move in.

3 Ts: You've begged your parents not to turn your bedroom
at home into an office, just in case.

Throw in the Towel

*"I am so over my roommate! I've tried everything, including talking to my
RA, but still things have not improved. I'm wasting what's supposed to
be a fun time in my life on trying to get along with someone who won't
cooperate. It's not worth it."*

—GREG, AGE 18

It takes a lot of work and effort to get along with someone you're at
odds with all the time, but simply not liking a person is not a good

enough reason to call it quits. Residence life staff considers changing roommates to be a last resort because if the real issue is that you
haven't learned how to get along with other people, then your problems will follow you to the next situation.

If you're fighting over personality differences or a lack of communication, you really have to earn your way out. That means exhausting
every avenue to clear up misunderstandings, communicating directly
and assertively with your roommate, examining your own contribu-
tions to the situation, asking your RA for help, and adjusting your
expectations.

If you've made every possible effort and nothing has changed,
you may be wondering, when is it enough? If you've reached a point
where the energy you're investing into resolving the conflict out-
weighs what you can reasonably expect in return, it's time to end it.

Situations You Should Not Ignore

Deciding when the scale tips in favor of quitting will be different for each person. However, there are situations that you should
never ignore:

- Threats of physical harm or behavior that you consider to
  jeopardize your personal safety
- Invasion of privacy, including computer hacking, identity
  theft, or tampering with your personal items
- Stealing
- Activities that are illegal or against university policy that could
  cause you to be kicked out or prosecuted as an accessory

If you've tried to address these issues on your own, sought the support of your RA, and the situation is escalating or persisting, it's time to end it. Don't take "no" for an answer. Insist that the university place you in another living situation or remove your roommate.

Going Your Separate Ways

If you've reached the point of calling it quits, you may not ever want to speak to your roommate again. But it's important to end it in a way that won't cause even more bad feelings. No matter what happened, make it your goal to head out the door with class and dignity. Depending on the size of your campus or the number of mutual friends, you may run into each other again. If you don't end it well, you could be feeling the repercussions for some time. While it may be tempting to pack up and leave without saying goodbye or to leave a nasty letter detailing all your roommate's faults, doing so will only add to the animosity.

By this time, you should have already had plenty of conversations about your disagreements. Saying goodbye is not the time to bring up the past, make a jab, pass judgment, or assign blame. Nothing is going to change at this point, so why bother? You don't have to lie and pretend you like the person if you don't, but at the same time, you don't need to create an enemy for life either.

How to Scrape the Ice

Ending on as positive a note as possible is in your own best interest since it allows you to move on without holding on to bitterness and resentment. Here are some ways you can say goodbye to your roommate without making things worse:

1. "It's too bad things didn't work out, but I wish you the best."
2. "There's a good chance we'll see each other around campus, so I hope we can still be friendly."
3. "We have a lot of mutual friends, classes together, etc. I don't want to avoid each other or feel weird just because things didn't work out."
4. "Now that we're putting an end to this situation, I hope we can end any bad feelings too."

Taking the high road while you're saying goodbye will help both of you focus on what's important now: moving on to better situations. Wrong or right, the past is the past. If you choose to continue to dwell on it now, you'll have only yourself to blame.

Hello—That Happened Five Months Ago!

Despite your efforts to end on a positive note, your roommate may try to bring you down. Some people wait until the end to say what they really feel, because they know they have nothing to lose. But there is a lot to lose if you let things get ugly. Both of you may say things you'll regret later and can never erase. If your roommate starts going down a bad road or makes accusations, do not engage. End the conversation quickly and politely, and then make your exit.

Don't Let 'Em Drag Ya Down

Again, nothing is going to change now, so it does no good to rehash old arguments. Here's how you can respond to a roommate who is determined to go down fighting:

1. "My goal is to end this on a positive note. I've said all I need to say and I wish you the best."
2. "We already agreed that this isn't working out, so I'd rather not get into it again. I hope things go well with your new roommate."
3. "All I wanted to say is goodbye and I hope everything works out for you."
4. "I don't want to cause any more bad feelings, so I'm going to leave now."
5. "I think we're past all this. Maybe when things calm down we can hang out again."

Remember that you can't control how your roommate is going to react or end things. Even if you and your roommate had irreconcilable differences, ending the living situation can still be very emotional and sad. This is particularly true if you started out as friends. While you may be overjoyed to get rid of your roommate, there can also be some feelings of failure or regret. Don't be hard on yourself or your roommate during the transition.

Forgive and Forget?

"My old roommate moved out last semester, but I'm still mad at her. She said some things about me that weren't true and she went behind my back several times. What really makes me mad is that she knows she was wrong, but she never said she was sorry. When I see her on campus I head in the other direction because just the sight of her makes me want to puke."

—ERICA, AGE 21

If you're feeling hurt or angry over what happened between you and your roommate, it may seem impossible to think about forgiving her. People often refuse to forgive because it's their way of punishing the other person. But does the other person burn with your anger, feel the knot in your stomach, or become distracted with your thoughts of old conversations playing over and over again in your mind? Holding grudges only causes self-inflicted pain.

Forgiveness is not something the other person earns; it's a choice you make. By choosing to forgive, you're not saying that everything that happened is okay or that you will ever forget. It takes a lot of energy to stay mad. What are you missing out on in the present by focusing on the past? Physically, your old roommate may not be sharing your room, but in your mind, he is getting free rent. As long as you choose to stay mad, you choose to let your former roommate have power over you.

How to Start Forgiving Your Old Roommate

Your decision to forgive and move on should not be contingent upon receiving an apology. The other person doesn't have to know of your forgiveness or even be present in your life. When you feel you're ready, here are steps that may make it easier:

1. Recognize that forgiveness is a choice you make for yourself, not the other person. It does not excuse the past, nor require that you forget.

2. Make a list of things your roommate did that you want to let go of or forgive. Give yourself the chance to fully process your feelings.

3. Acknowledge your part. Were you honest? Did you speak up when and how you needed to? Did you ever antagonize your roommate? Own up to your responsibility, and if necessary, forgive yourself too.

4. Consider what you gained from the relationship. Even though it was rough, did you learn anything about yourself? Are you a stronger person now? Have you built new awareness and skills?

5. Write a letter to the person **that you will not mail.** In your letter, say everything you feel, including acknowledgement of your part in the relationship and what you gained. Tell the person you forgive her and how that benefits you.

6. Create a ceremony in which you will get rid of the letter, like burying it, ripping it up, or cutting it into tiny pieces. Imagine releasing the person's hold on you as you symbolically destroy what you've put on paper.

Bitterness is a heavy burden to carry. Forgiving your roommate, and yourself if necessary, gives you your life back. Reward yourself by focusing on your own happiness and well-being.

I Said I Was Sorry, What More Do You Want?

When you're angry with someone, it's easy to point the finger of blame in the other direction. But once you step back from the situation, you may discover that you're the one who needs to apologize. You are certainly not responsible for 100 percent of the problem, just as your roommate is not. It took two of you to create the issue, and being big enough to acknowledge your part is a mature sign of good will. Just like forgiveness, being accountable for your actions benefits you in the end. It makes you feel less like a victim, relieves feelings of guilt (if you have any), and gives you the peace of mind that you did all you could.

A warning though: Do not apologize with the expectation of having it reciprocated. Just because you say you're sorry does not mean your roommate feels the same way. That's okay; this is about you and what you need to do.

How to Say I'm Sorry

Hopefully, apologizing will ease some tension and make the split more positive, but if not, you will know that you did the right thing. If you're ready to take the step forward with an apology, here are some ways you can say it:

1. "I realize that I'm partly responsible for what happened and I'm sorry."
2. "I'm partly to blame for what happened, and I'm sorry I let it continue."
3. "I know I'm not always the easiest person to room with, so I'm sorry for the times I made it difficult."
4. "I'm sure that I played a role in what happened and I acknowledge that."
5. "I know I did some things that added to the situation and I apologize."
6. "I'm sorry for anything I did that made things worse."

Acknowledging your part in the breakdown can be very empowering. It allows you to recognize what to do differently in the future so that you are less likely to have to relive the same situation with the next roommate.

My Roommate Won't Accept My Apology

It would be nice if your roommate listened to your apology, accepted it, then acknowledged his own faults, but it doesn't always work out that way. Again, don't apologize just so you can hear the other person say, "I'm sorry." It comes across as insincere and manipulative. If the rift between the two of you is deep, it may take time to forgive one another; that doesn't lessen the impact of what you have to say. Sometimes apologies take awhile to sink in, so give it time.

Actions, Not Words

"Sorry" is just a word without meaning until it's put into action. Someone who is truly sorry is committed to behaving differently in the future and does not try to justify the past, so put your words into action. For example, if you used to gossip about your roommate, stop it immediately. Here's how you can respond if your roommate rejects your peace offering:

1. "Even if you can't accept my apology now, I hope you'll be able to in the future."
2. "I was hoping you could accept what I have to say, but even if that's not possible, it doesn't change how I feel."
3. "Please keep in mind what I said because I really do mean it."

4. "I know that what I have to say may sound empty unless you see it in action."
5. "Whether you accept my apology or not, it still stands."
6. "I don't expect you to believe what I'm saying right now; maybe it will take some time."

Now take those words and put them into action. You don't need your roommate's acceptance to do the right thing—do it for yourself.

Moving On

Okay, it's done, finished, over with. Now it's time for you to move on! Whether you have a new roommate or get a private room, you'll need to make some changes in order to put this behind you. The best predictor of future behavior is past behavior (that's why your SAT scores matter). In other words, unless you do something to change, it's very likely that you'll wind up repeating your past. The biggest thing you can change is to stop talking about what happened in a negative way. If people ask you why you changed rooms, just say, "Things didn't work out." If you go on and on about how horrible it was, you'd only be broadcasting that you are potentially hard to get along with. Negativity attracts negativity. There's no need to bad-mouth your former roommate and keep old issues alive. It's time to let go. So if negative thoughts keep creeping in, replace them with positive thoughts and you'll feel a lot more productive.

Tips to Remember

- You have to earn your way out of a roommate dispute by exhausting every avenue of communication. Unless you can honestly say you've tried everything, it's not over.
- If your situation involves risk of personal safety, invasion of privacy, stealing, or illegal activities and your concerns are not *immediately* addressed, move.
- Do everything you can to end things on a positive or at least a neutral note.
- Forgiveness is a choice you make for yourself, not the other person. It doesn't mean you excuse past wrongs or forget what happened. It allows you to let go of resentment and bitterness so that you can move on.
- Apologizing for your part in creating the problem or for what you might have done to keep it alive means that you acknowledge you're not a victim.
- When it's over, put things in the past unless you want to keep reliving it. Negativity attracts negativity.

Visit your campus counseling center or read tips on how to say goodbye on the University of Buffalo's counseling services Web site at *www.ub-counseling.buffalo.edu*.

For articles and resources on forgiving, visit *www.forgivenessweb.com.* To learn how to focus on the positive side, check out two books by Dr. Martin Selgiman: *Learned Optimism: How to Change Your Mind and Your Life* (Free Press, 1998) and *Authentic Happiness* (Free Press, 2002).

14

Dealing with Stress

Quick Quiz: True or False

People are constantly telling you to lay off the
caffeine even when you haven't had any.   T/F

You have stomach cramps, but the health center
can't find anything wrong.   T/F

If someone looks at you the wrong way, it can
ruin your whole day.   T/F

Score

1 T: You have no fingernails left since you've chewed them
down as far as possible.

2 Ts: You're broke since you've spent all your money on
aspirin.

3 Ts: You used to be a lot more fun.

Stressed to the Max

*"Ever since I've been dealing with my roommate issue, I've had the worst
headaches. I feel on edge and have a hard time relaxing. It's affecting my
concentration too. Even one of my professors mentioned it to me."*

—JILL, AGE 21

Dealing with roommate issues on top of everything else in college
can be stressful and can take a toll on you physically and emotionally.
Whether you decide to stay with your roommate or part ways, you are
bound to feel stressed out by the entire situation.

Each of us defines and reacts to stress differently. Receiving a speeding ticket is enough for some people to become frantic with worry, while others couldn't care less. Some people are totally stressed and you wouldn't know it because they've checked out mentally.

Not all stress is bad though. We need some stress in our lives or else we wouldn't be able to function! So the goal is not to live a stress-free life, but to learn how to maintain stress at a healthy, productive level. Biologically, our bodies handle stress with a fight or flight response, which is an automatic reaction in which our body is ready to fight the danger (stressor) or flee from it. The surge of adrenaline is designed to help us survive in the moment, but prolonged stress keeps us in this heightened state of awareness and can cause long-term negative effects, like headaches, ulcers, and impaired concentration.

Symptoms of Stress Overload

If you've lived with stress so long you're not sure what's considered a normal level, here are signs that you've hit overload:

- Racing heart and/or sweaty palms
- Feeling angry, irritable, or tense
- Irregular sleep and/or eating habits
- Headaches
- Tightness of the chest, neck, jaw, and back muscles
- Skin breakouts
- Stomach cramps or indigestion
- Shallow breathing
- Cold hands and/or feet (due to poor circulation)
- Being easily startled

All of these symptoms are signs that your body is no longer able to process the amount of stress it's exposed to and that you need to get some help in managing your load.

Stop the Stress Cycle!

Even though stress is defined differently for each of us, it occurs in the same cycle. Once you become aware of it, you can interrupt the pattern by changing your thoughts and choosing different behavior.

The cycle starts with a triggering event like your roommate leaving a pile of dirty clothes in the middle of the room. How you think determines how you feel. An example is your thinking, "Why should I have to deal with this?" Your thoughts lead to your emotions, which in this case may be anger, pain, or frustration. Based on your emotions, you choose a behavior. This is your way of expressing your emotions and could be anything from kicking the clothes, to picking up the clothes, to ignoring them. So, the cycle again is: triggering event, thoughts, emotions, and behavior.

You can see that not everyone would have the same reaction to the event, and that's why each person defines stress differently. In fact, the event doesn't matter since you can't control it. What matters is how you choose to think and react.

Let Go of What You Can't Control

The first step in interrupting the stress cycle is acknowledging what you can and cannot control. Focusing on things you can't control is an extremely stressful thought pattern because it makes you feel helpless.

On a piece of paper, write down everything that's stressing you out right now. Not only roommate issues, but everything—papers due, student loans, your parents, car trouble, anything. Fill up the entire page if necessary. When you've got it all down, take a good hard look at what you've written and honestly ask yourself what's within your control and what isn't. Cross out everything on your list that you can't control. (Hint: you can't control other people.) What's left? If you've crossed out the majority of stuff on your list, you know that you have a tendency to focus on things you can't do anything about anyway. However, you always have control over your own reactions.

Now, take out a clean sheet of paper and write down only the items that you can control. You can't address everything at once, so the next step is to prioritize your list. What's the most important item? If you answered, "everything," then you're into another stressful thought pattern: all or nothing thinking. This is when you believe that if you can't do it all perfectly, then it's better to do nothing. But procrastination causes even more stress! So, force yourself to number your list by either tackling the easiest item, or choosing the item that, if addressed, will have the greatest impact. Wad up that first piece of paper and throw it away! It will feel good to release it.

Pour It out on Paper

"My friend gave me a journal, but I have no idea what to write. I don't want to re-live all my problems, so I don't see how writing about them will help."

—JEANNETTE, AGE 20

Journaling is an excellent way to release pent-up emotions and reduce stress. Unlike a diary, journaling is not a daily account of your life; it's a resource to use whenever you need it. Think of it as an emotional purge. There are no rules, spelling and punctuation doesn't count, it can be handwritten or typed, and you can say anything you want. In fact, that's the goal—say anything and everything on your mind, no matter how nasty. It's much safer to release that kind of stuff privately on paper than to share it with the person you had in mind. If you need help getting started, here are some ideas and exercises to prompt you:

> What I really want to happen is . . .
> What I'm most afraid of is . . .
> The main thing on my mind is . . .
> If I could change one thing about my life it would be . . .
> What I really want to say and can't is . . .
> I would feel so much better if . . .
> What I am most grateful for is . . .
> My life would improve if I knew how to . . .

Journaling helps you figure things out by letting you see it in black and white. It provides some distance so that you can put things in perspective. Finally, journaling will help you become more aware of the internal dialogue running through your head and even stuff that you didn't know was bothering you until you started writing.

Take a Deep Breath

"Sometimes my chest feels tight and I have trouble breathing. I run out of breath just walking across campus. I know it's related to stress because I never had this problem until this semester. I signed up for a yoga class and it's helping."

—ANGIE, AGE 18

You may think you already know how to breathe properly; after all, you're doing it right now. But when stressed, we tend to take short, shallow breaths, reducing the intake of oxygen and the release of carbon dioxide. Improper breathing leaves us less equipped to deal with stressful situations and contributes to anxiety, panic attacks, muscle tension, headaches, and fatigue.

Typically we breathe in one of two patterns: chest breathing or abdominal breathing. When you breathe with your chest, which many of us do when stressed, the breathing is shallow, often irregular, and rapid. When air is inhaled, the chest expands and the shoulders rise. Some people even hold their breath, experience shortness of breath, or hyperventilate. This also leads to poor circulation causing cold feet and/or hands.

Abdominal breathing is a deep, natural, unrestricted pattern using the diaphragm, a sheet-like muscle separating the lungs and the abdomen. You experience it when you have a big yawn. (In fact, triggering yourself to yawn is an instant stress reliever.) When you inhale, the diaphragm expands, filling your lungs with oxygen. When you exhale, the diaphragm contracts, removing carbon dioxide.

If you do one thing to reduce your stress, learn to use abdominal breathing. It sounds simple, but the effects are profound. You can do it anywhere, anytime, without anyone else knowing. It doesn't require equipment and it's free!

Abdominal Breathing

Here are a few exercises to get you started. Once you master the technique, you'll be able to fall into the pattern within seconds, whether you're standing, sitting, or lying down:

1. Lie down on the floor with knees bent and feet flat. Place your hands on your abdomen, about three inches down from your belly button.
2. Breathe in through your nose and feel your abdomen rise. You will feel your lungs fill with air and your chest rise slightly.
3. Exhale through your mouth and feel your abdomen sink back down. Notice how your body releases more and more tension every time you exhale.
4. Repeat the pattern at least ten times.

If you've been conditioned to breathe incorrectly, the exercise can feel a little strange at first. Also, breathing puts us in touch with emotions we may have "stuffed." If emotions or stressful thoughts about money, exams, or roommate problems come up, just continue the exercise and pretend you're releasing the problem each time you exhale. Here are some alternate breathing exercises:

1. Repeat as before, but after inhaling, hold for a count of four and then exhale. This helps to increase lung capacity and slow down your heart rate.

2. Reverse the abdominal breathing process by contracting when you inhale and expanding when you exhale. It takes so much concentration and focus to go against the normal breathing pattern that there is no room for any stressful, distracting thoughts.

More Ways to De-Stress

There are tons of ways people attempt to relax, but not all of them are healthy. Smoking, drinking alcohol or caffeinated drinks, and eating junk food may make you feel good for the moment, but actually cause the opposite effect. Caffeine, nicotine, sugar, and alcohol spike your adrenaline level, but then leaves you feeling drained when it drops. As alternatives, here are twenty-five healthy ways to de-stress and re-energize. These ideas won't change your situation, but they will give you a chance to relax and regroup.

25 Stress Busters

1. Exercise.
2. Listen to your favorite music.
3. Visit a pet store and play with a kitten or puppy.
4. Read a book for pleasure.
5. Take a shower.
6. Rent or go to a movie.
7. Call a friend.

8. Go to a park.

9. Visit a museum.

10. Blow bubbles.

11. Go to a ballgame and scream.

12. Light some candles.

13. Take a nap.

14. Plan your spring break or summer vacation. Read the brochures often.

15. Buy some playdough, balloons, or a Slinky.

16. Take a yoga class.

17. Go for a hike.

18. Read the comics.

19. Buy some packing bubble wrap and pop all the bubbles.

20. Play your favorite video game.

21. Buy a 64-count box of crayons and color.

22. Get some old vacation posters. Put them up near your bed and daydream.

23. Release upper body tension by rolling your shoulders forward, up, backward, and down. Repeat several times, and then reverse the roll.

24. Go to a batting cage.

25. Make chocolate chip cookies (or just eat the cookie dough).

Lighten Up

When was the last time you had a really good laugh? Sometimes a situation is so stressful, you're left with only two choices: to laugh or cry. Why not laugh? Humor is a great stress reliever (and it will make you a lot more fun to be around too). So if you can't beat them, join them! Here are seven ways to add a little humor to your life:

Seven Ways to Add Humor to Your Life

1. See your situation through the eyes of a professional comedian and exaggerate or distort it to a ridiculous point. If your roommate snores, imagine the walls shaking, alarms going off, and the whole building crumbling.

2. Imagine how the characters on your favorite TV comedy show might handle your situation. What would it be like if your life was an episode of *The Simpsons, Bernie Mac, Saturday Night Live,* or *Punk'd?*

3. Create a humor folder containing funny pictures, cards, cartoons, quotes, and stories that make you smile. Be on the lookout for examples of humor, adding to your folder often. Look at it any time you need some comic relief.

4. Check out the American Film Institute's suggestions for the 100 funniest movies at *www.afi.com.* Rent and watch at least one comedy a week.

5. Go to a card shop and read all the humorous greeting cards.

6. Buy a whoopie cushion from *www.fartmart.com.* The same company also sells fart spray, the Remote Controlled Electronic Fart Machine, and the Pull My Finger Fart CD.

7. Sign up to receive a daily e-mail joke at *www.ahajokes.com.*

Notice the types of people and opportunities you attract the more you de-stress and lighten up. People who are having fun in their lives are a magnet for more positive, healthy relationships.

Tips to Remember

- We all experience stress, but in different ways. What is stressful for one person may not faze another.
- Stress occurs in the same cycle: triggering event, thoughts, feelings, and behavior. Once you become aware of the pattern, you can interrupt it and change your outcome.
- Focusing on things you can't control (like other people) makes you feel helpless and more stressed. You can begin to make positive changes by focusing on what is within your control.
- Journaling is a safe way to express your deepest thoughts and emotions. There are no rules, just the freedom to be honest.
- Choose healthy ways to relieve stress. Nicotine, alcohol, caffeine and junk food may make you feel good for the moment, but will leave you feeling drained and sluggish.
- Humor is a great stress reliever. Finding ways to laugh at your situation will put you in control, rather than the situation controlling you.

You can get more information about managing stress from the American Institute of Stress at *www.stress.org*. To learn more about breathing, meditation, visualization, and other relaxation techniques, read *The Relaxation and Stress Reduction Workbook, 5th edition* (New Harbinger, 2000).

Index

About the Author

SUSAN FEE is a licensed counselor, life coach, corporate trainer, and freelance writer. She is also adjunct faculty at several colleges, where she teaches interpersonal communication, public speaking, psychology, and critical thinking. She can be reached at *www.susanfee.com*.